FROM
TAILSPIN
TO
TAILWIND

BUDDY
TEASTER

FROM
TAILSPIN
TO
TAILWIND

LEADERSHIP LESSONS
FOR TURNING CRISIS
INTO CLARITY

Copyright © 2025 by Buddy Teaster.

All rights reserved. No part of this book may be used or reproduced in any manner whatsoever without prior written consent of the author, except as provided by the United States of America copyright law.

Published by Advantage Books, Charleston, South Carolina.
An imprint of Advantage Media.

ADVANTAGE is a registered trademark, and the Advantage colophon is a trademark of Advantage Media Group, Inc.

Printed in the United States of America.

10 9 8 7 6 5 4 3 2 1

ISBN: 979-8-89188-181-5 (Hardcover)
ISBN: 979-8-89188-183-9 (eBook)

Library of Congress Control Number: 2025906539

Cover design by Matthew Morse.
Layout design by Lance Buckley.

This publication is designed to provide accurate and authoritative information in regard to the subject matter covered. It is sold with the understanding that the publisher is not engaged in rendering legal, accounting, or other professional services. If legal advice or other expert assistance is required, the services of a competent professional person should be sought.

Advantage Books is an imprint of Advantage Media Group. Advantage Media helps busy entrepreneurs, CEOs, and leaders write and publish a book to grow their business and become the authority in their field. Advantage authors comprise an exclusive community of industry professionals, idea-makers, and thought leaders. For more information go to **advantagemedia.com.**

For David and Robert

CONTENTS

INTRODUCTION ... 1
Navigating the Storm

CHAPTER 1 ... 7
Getting Up to Speed

CHAPTER 2 ... 25
Surviving Self-Inflicted Wounds and Unforeseen Loss

CHAPTER 3 ... 37
Strategy and Results

CHAPTER 4 ... 45
Core Values = Culture

CHAPTER 5 ... 61
Clarifying the Mission and Setting a Vision

CHAPTER 6 ... 73
Implementing a Robust Operating System

CHAPTER 7 ... 87
Building a Strong Team

CHAPTER 8 103

Our Secret Weapon: A Committed Board

CHAPTER 9 123

Cultivating Great Partnerships

CHAPTER 10 155

Powering Change and Growth

CHAPTER 11 173

Following a North Star

CONCLUSION 185

Finding the Updrafts

ACKNOWLEDGMENT 189

ABOUT THE AUTHOR 191

GLOSSARY 193

INTRODUCTION

Navigating the Storm

It looked so good at the beginning. A new approach to a problem, industry enthusiasm, millions of dollars in funding, good PR. And it took off like a rocket ship. Success led to success.

I'm not talking about a high-tech start-up or a new weight loss drug but the founding of Soles4Souls (S4S). The first few years were, by all accounts, remarkable. But all was not as rosy as it seemed. Soon, the rocket ship ran out of fuel, the good press morphed into investigative reporting, and let's just say the industry enthusiasm cooled rapidly.

Like real physics, the same forces that launched S4S into orbit also put it in an existential nosedive. This might seem a little theatrical, but it's how it felt at the time. This is the story of the journey from that tailspin to finding S4S's tailwind.

You might be asking what S4S is. We are a 501(c)3 nonprofit organization, creating opportunities for people through shoes and clothing. Based in Nashville, Tennessee, we have about eighty employees spread across half a dozen countries and more than twenty states. As we often say, we are small but mighty!

The roots of this organization are in disaster relief, but we're far more than that today. We focus on repurposing shoes and clothes to create economic, health, educational, service, and environmental opportunities. S4S was launched with a simple vision and a noble purpose. But five years after S4S was officially founded in 2006, the organization seemed to have lost its way. Things didn't seem simple or, frankly, noble.

S4S was in a tailspin.

In 2012, the organization faced multiple serious obstacles, any one of which might have been enough to make us crash and burn. When I arrived as S4S's new CEO in October of that year, after a career that included experience in the for-profit and not-for-profit worlds, our reputation was in the tank, and bankruptcy appeared imminent. Every metric that mattered was going in the wrong direction. On my very first day, as I was meeting everyone on the S4S staff, I asked them, "What's going on?" The answer that stood out to me was from an employee named Nicole. She said, "I'll tell you what's going on. My nana called me and said, 'I give money to you people. What in the hell are you doing down there?'" When someone's grandmother calls to chew her out about the place she works, you don't just have a reputational problem; you have a very personal problem. From the moment I walked in the door, it was clear that we were going to have to fix almost everything about S4S.

While there's no agreement on who first used the quip "Never let a good crisis go to waste," it was certainly on my mind as I left the office that day. Clearly, what had started with so much momentum wasn't working. With a glass-half-full mindset, I saw the opportunity to change anything and everything. Right away, I knew we had to start talking honestly to each other about the why, the who, and the how of S4S. Over the years, by creating a shared sense of what was possible, we turned our biggest tests into our most important lessons.

We've done our best to answer Nicole's nana. In 2024, we distributed more than 5.7 million pairs of shoes and 3.98 million pieces of apparel around the world, diverting 9.2 million pounds of potential waste from landfills while generating $69,549,921 in economic impact in the places we served. So, I don't think tailspin to turnaround is hyperbole.

A part of the tailspin had to do with failing to provide transparent details so that the public, and our employees, understood the organization's mission and the mechanics underpinning the operation. When those failures, among others, became public through an April 2011 investigative article published in Nashville's daily newspaper—the article that made Nicole's nana call her—they triggered another disaster; the reputational kind. This book details far more than how we went about transforming S4S's reputation. I will talk in detail about how we used an entrepreneurial attitude, business discipline, and a focus on our mission to move from aspirational ideas about a better world to a high-functioning organization that delivers results that matter to those we serve. Our journey has been from disruption to opportunity, and that's the spirit of *From Tailspin to Tailwind*. It is a story about the power of resilience in the face of adversity. This book examines how a struggling organization overcame significant challenges through innovative approaches, strong values, and effective partnerships. It highlights S4S's journey from dealing with crisis to becoming a thriving organization and emphasizes the importance of adaptability, collaboration, and shared leadership. We'll dive into strategies for transformation and growth by focusing on things like defining and living core values and a mission, implementing a robust operating system, building strong teams and a committed board, and developing strategic partnerships that fuel growth.

It is by applying such strategies intentionally and consistently that we now feel a tailwind pushing us into the future. I'm so proud of what everyone associated with S4S—team members, the board, partners, volunteers, and donors—has done to get us back to altitude and soaring once again.

LESSONS, NOT SERMONS: N = 1

One thing to share that is key to understanding me generally and this book specifically: I don't pretend to have the answers. I only know the decisions and approaches that worked for us. For years I was an ultra-runner. This means mostly running distances of fifty kilometers or more, including a lot of fifty-mile and several hundred-mile races. I was a regular reader of a column called "N = 1" in *Ultra Running* magazine. N = 1 means a sample of one. When you're running fifty or a hundred miles, you don't get a chance to practice those full distances very often, so you're always looking for informed advice that you can use. And this guy's column was very smart, coming from the position of "Look, I have no idea if this applies to you. This is my training and this is what worked or didn't work for me. But I don't know if it will work for you in your race, on that day, in those conditions." Everything in this book is N = 1. I don't know if it's going to relate to your exact circumstances, but I hope that some of it will and that the rest can inspire you to form new ideas. I'm not trying to be prescriptive, to give you a formula for success. The stories and lessons in *From Tailspin to Tailwind* chronicle the things that we went through and the strategies we applied. I hope you'll take all our experiences in the spirit of N = 1.

From Tailspin to Tailwind acknowledges how much work, luck, and time it takes to transform a failing organization, as well as telling the stories of how new challenges constantly emerge—including, in our case, mourning the loss of people who were instrumental in building our organization. Then, there's the even harder task of finding inspiration in their example, so that we can grow and improve in their absence. It is my intent that this book offers pragmatic approaches that any business or organization can use if they're struggling to emerge from a trying set of circumstances.

Your version of a tailspin will be different from ours. Tailspins can look different in large organizations than in small ones, where the margin between success and failure might be measured in weeks. When facing a reputational crisis, a leadership vacuum, a market shift, or a financial catastrophe, organizations of any size can find themselves in crisis, leading to knee-jerk decisions that accelerate the tailspin. So often, one crisis leads to another. Sometimes, you don't even see the problem until things have grown from a small spark to a full-blown fire. I'm mixing metaphors, but you get the idea. It's hard to get out of a tailspin.

I hope you can learn from our experiences. Through features titled "Another Voice" in each chapter, you'll hear from others who have contributed to harnessing the tailwind that continues to increase the impact S4S has on so many lives.

Perhaps you run a business or lead an organization that's caught in a tailspin and you share the feeling we had in 2012 that "It can't get much worse, so what have we got to lose by trying?" Maybe you're an entrepreneur just getting started or trying to keep the plane level as you battle the energizing but dangerous wind shear of rapid growth. Maybe you see the glimmers of a future crisis on the horizon and want to strengthen your organization to stave it off. Wherever you are, I hope that what we've learned at S4S might provide you with lessons that can help you get, and stay, airborne.

CHAPTER 1
Getting Up to Speed

Because context matters, let me start this story of transformation from tailspin to tailwind with a nutshell version of what S4S is and what it does, and also convey why the organization was in free fall in 2012. My interest is in linking that complicated past to the bright present by sharing the things we did that enabled us to "regain altitude." That's the real story I want to tell. That's the story that might help you map your way out of crisis or navigate from crisis to clarity.

In 2018, six years into my tenure as the CEO of S4S, I wrote *Shoestrings*, a book that chronicled the first steps of our transformative journey. For the most part, where that book ends is where this one begins. By 2018, not only had we finally climbed out of crisis management mode; we had evolved our mission from "Changing the World One Pair at a Time" to "Wearing Out Poverty," and we were back in the black financially. We were focused on the entire organization living by the values represented in the acronym we had settled on to explain how we wanted to approach our work and treat everyone in our ecosystem: TEAM.

Transparent
Entrepreneurial
Accountable
Meaningful

The story that still needed to be told after *Shoestrings* was twofold: one, how we put TEAM into practice, and two, how we met new

7

challenges with a mix of steadfast values and new capabilities. If *Shoestrings* was essentially the story of survival and an explanation of our approach to reducing poverty, the goal of this book is to chronicle how we became more adaptive, collaborative, and innovative. There will be plenty of stories that bring those changes to life, and how could there not be when S4S is blessed with an abundance of inspiring, innovative partners working in what most of us would see as impossible situations?

Before I show you how we got out of our free fall, let me tell you a little bit more about S4S.

FROM NATURAL DISASTERS TO MANMADE CALAMITIES

The beginning of Soles4Souls is rooted in the events that occurred on December 26, 2004, in the Indian Ocean. A 9.2–9.3 magnitude earthquake spawned a tsunami that slammed into the west coast of Sumatra, Indonesia, killing nearly 230,000 people and displacing more than 1.7 million in fourteen countries around the region. The three founders of what would become S4S (one of whom—Wayne Elsey—came from the footwear industry) watched the coverage with heartache. Elsey was particularly haunted by a photograph of a single shoe left on a beach by the retreating tidal wave. Wanting to help those whose lives were torn apart by the tsunami, the three men organized a shoe drive. They collected a couple of hundred thousand pairs of shoes, shipped them to Indonesia, and succeeded in getting them distributed to those in need.

Less than a year later, Hurricane Katrina struck New Orleans. This time, Elsey, his colleagues, and hundreds of volunteers collected and distributed more than 750,000 pairs of shoes. Before long, S4S formally incorporated as a nonprofit. By 2010, S4S had become known for crisis response, which it put to full effect when a 7.0 magnitude earthquake literally flattened parts of Haiti.

By 2012, S4S had collected and distributed over thirty million pairs of new and gently used shoes to people in need and a similarly impressive amount of clothing (and these numbers have grown exponentially in the years since).

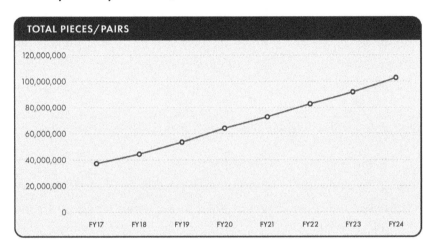

Parallel to its disaster relief efforts, S4S gradually evolved to include providing microentrepreneurs in low-income countries with shoes and clothes—products that are always in demand—to create small businesses that could help them and their communities escape the grip of poverty. Totally redefined and entirely transparent today, the core idea of microentrepreneurship in 2010 was the same: to provide experienced partners on the ground in impoverished places around the globe with high-quality used shoes and apparel so that local entrepreneurs could sell them at affordable prices. We have not only transformed this model but renamed it 4Opportunity—a name that goes to the heart of how the program works, by creating *opportunity* for people to improve their standard of living—and that's the nomenclature I will use from this point on. The entrepreneurs S4S works with benefit financially while providing practical products that contribute to their customers' safety, health, and personal dignity. Rather than only providing relief after natural disasters, supporting 4Opportunity entrepreneurs has increased S4S's impact in helping more people lift themselves out of poverty. A key reason is the nominal prices we charge for the products we provide to our direct partners. The revenue from those sales earns enough to cover collection, logistics, and labor costs, which significantly contributes to our organization's sustainability. Because our prices are so low, our partners and the entrepreneurs they support can earn a meaningful income. Then, they plow that back into community improvements such as building schools or medical clinics, teaching workers new skills, and providing clean water supplies and better nutrition.

Selling shoes to entrepreneurs in the developing world is a hard concept to explain in a soundbite. We needed to address the kinds of questions we heard regularly: "Are nonprofits supposed to sell things?" "Why don't you give them the shoes for free?" "What do you mean my donations go outside the US?" S4S's leadership didn't clarify how that model worked to the public—or to its employees—failing to explain or contextualize the "selling" part. Most people fill in the blanks themselves, however inaccurately, when communication is vague, and this led to a serious backlash when the truth came out. What should have been a shining example of a better model for helping people get out of poverty instead got lost in innuendo, accusation, and ego. We'll come back to this—because it was from these depths that S4S rebounded.

The most important part of S4S's journey was in this evolution. What started as a disaster relief organization is today a recognized pioneer of the nonprofit social enterprise model. In 2024, our vision—breaking the cycle of poverty in the very communities it grips most tightly, providing relief, lifting up homeless youth, and doing good for the planet—is at work around the globe. Since 2006, we have distributed shoes domestically and in more than 139 countries. We still distribute new shoes for free to people in need, but that's just one facet of the work we undertake toward the wider goals of

- creating opportunity,
- serving those in need, and
- protecting the environment.

If we stopped the S4S story in 2009, or leapfrogged to 2018, the organization would look like an unqualified success.

But that's not how time works.

After its formal incorporation in 2006, S4S began its shift toward supporting microenterprise in developing countries. It did so, however, without fully informing its stakeholders: the shoe donors, volunteers, and even staff who coordinated shoe drives to secure donations. But a 2009 investigative report in *The Tennessean*, the newspaper serving our hometown of Nashville, told everyone—describing the much-loved charity as "a middleman." And it said far more. The reporting raised concerns about Elsey's salary and close ties to the shoe industry. *The Tennessean*'s 2009 reporting also noted the incongruence of having the charity's CEO as its board chair. While this is common practice in the for-profit world, the nonprofit universe sees it as a potential hindrance to the board's first duty: scrutinizing the operation through independent eyes. In many cases, even having the CEO on the board is considered poor governance, let alone as chair.

Sixteen months later, *The Tennessean* published another exposé, this one focused on the practice of selling shoes to microentrepreneurs and implying that donations were not going to charity. Over a year had passed between the investigations. S4S could have spent those months educating supporters about how its model worked and how microenterprise created far greater economic impact in impoverished communities than simply giving away products. Perhaps S4S leadership feared people would stop donating. Perhaps they feared still-closer scrutiny. Whatever the rationale, the failure to put S4S's house in order dealt a devastating blow to the public perception of the organization's work.

There was more, and it was a mess. A very tangled separate charity not controlled by the board, an insanely expensive lawsuit over a lease dispute, personal loans from organizational funds that almost broke the law ...

After months of public wrangling with *The Tennessean*, the organization backed down. But it was far too little, and much too late: The damage was done. Less than a year after *The Tennessean*'s second investigation, Elsey resigned, and a national search for his replacement began. Enter me. Enter Nicole's nana. Enter other employees such as Kelly Modena, who, as she recounted in *Shoestrings*, recalls asking the questions "Tell me what I'm doing here? Where are our shoes going?" She was on the frontline, encouraging people to donate shoes, and she didn't know what was happening?! The betrayal ran much deeper than I think anyone really understood.

In any business, including nonprofits, perception is everything. People who give time and money to causes they care about deserve to know, and we are responsible for showing them, that the people to whom they entrust these resources are good stewards. S4S's individual donors, volunteers, and staff learned about all the bad stuff not from S4S but in their Sunday morning newspapers. Their confidence wasn't merely shaken. It was shattered.

At least I could read about this before I accepted the job. And the board shared with me as much as they knew. However, it didn't take long to figure out that the fiscal picture was much worse than anyone suspected. The year before I came to the organization, S4S reported a loss of $2 million on revenue of $4 million. It had never been profitable, but that was hard to see in the audited financials. The management team, using generally accepted accounting principles (GAAP), viewed all product donated as gifts in kind (GIK) as revenue. This is the right way to do the accounting, but it can mask real problems, most notably what's happening with cash. Although common in the nonprofit world, this approach has no analog among for-profits because you have to put down sales as cash, not some totally arbitrary value. I had never heard of such a thing, and it blew my mind. That's because GIK *are not cash*. You can *turn them into* cash, but when you value a pair of shoes at $30, then sell them for $1, well—it's easy to see how no one really had a clear picture of how much money was gushing out of S4S. Another problem was that S4S "crept" from accepting shoes (and a little later, clothing) to accepting a diverse range of items—from wheelchairs to kitchen tile. Again, perfectly legitimate in terms of GAAP, but a veritable funhouse mirror that prevented us from getting a true picture of fiscal reality.

Beyond such financial and product concerns, when I was hired, two board members resigned; one because she wanted to bring my predecessor back and the other because he wanted to close the doors and liquidate the assets. They just didn't believe it could be fixed. I respect that both acted on their convictions, but their departure left the board with only three active members. Team members were disillusioned. The microenterprise model S4S touted was giving most of the profit to the middlemen, not the entrepreneurs. We didn't have true on-the-ground partners who understood local cultures, politics, and economics; and the reputational loss had sent many of the corporate partners scurrying.

CHANGE COURSE OR CRASH

In 2012, I didn't know if S4S's survival was possible. But I knew I wanted to try. There was an amazing idea at its core: using the best of capitalism to create opportunities for people to get out of poverty. By the end of 2013, we had cut the financial losses in half, refocused on our mission, created the tagline "Wearing Out Poverty," and begun to put the pieces in place to make that tagline a reality. A critical element of doing so was leaning into what we now label 4Opportunity.

Despite the myriad problems we unearthed, I was inspired by S4S's desire to help transform lives, the scale of the impact it had already accomplished, and the genuine passion people across the organization felt for its mission. While the lack of communication about the shift to an increased focus on microenterprise had helped to create the crisis and cement the appearance of impropriety in the public's mind, I saw the enormous potential to increase our impact if we did it right. To get there would require a reduction in our dependency on third parties, and it would demand full transparency. But the core idea was sound. Small businesses offer an ability to expand economic impact in the communities they serve, something like the concentric circles that grow outward from a pebble dropped into a pond. A pair of shoes given away can improve the life of the wearer; a pair of shoes sold at a price that is locally affordable can still improve the life of the wearer but will also improve the circumstances of the person who sold the shoes, those dependent on them, and conceivably, the businesses where that seller in turn will spend money. Teaching people to fish rather than simply giving them fish is a well-known principle for a reason.

The beginning of S4S's use of microenterprise dates to the organization's inception. Brothers Nelson and Paul Wilson were founding board members. They had experience with faith-based humanitarian outreach in Central America. After seeing success in sending shoes to natural disaster zones and facing a stockpile of donated used shoes, they saw an opportunity to help in the fight against poverty by partnering with missionaries they knew. The missionaries identified single mothers as the most effective conduit. These women began to set up little shoe shops on street corners. They would sell the used shoes S4S had collected, which allowed them to earn a good living. S4S fronted the women the first shipment of shoes, but they had to retain some profit from their sales to purchase the next shipment. As this approach spread to other countries, it continued to prove successful, but it eventually was mired in the controversy that had sent S4S into its tailspin. At the center of that controversy was a reality that people didn't fully understand: The fastest way to get donated products to potential buyers is by using for-profit distributors, which was the focus of the initial investigation conducted by *The Tennessean*. Internal differences in vision between the Wilson brothers and Elsey on the use of such distributors added to the problem.

Soles4Souls still responds to disasters with free, new shoes and clothes for people—and we always will—but it was through 4Opportunity that we could not only make the organization sustainable but also kickstart our own growth. If we were sincere about reducing poverty, 4Opportunity was how we would get there. Part of the value Elsey created at the outset was because of his contacts in the shoe industry. He was able to get shoe manufacturers to donate new shoes, often in large quantities. Sometimes models simply don't sell as predicted, or a product has quality control issues such as the wrong color or a piece of trim that comes loose. When donating, companies specify markets where their products cannot be sold (usually where they have a commercial presence), so in parts of the world that are fair game, entrepreneurs can purchase donated products from S4S and realize good margins while still selling at prices that are affordable to those in their communities. S4S continues to receive donations (both new and gently used shoes and clothing, as well as financial contributions) from individuals, shoe drives, and elsewhere, but the largest volume comes from corporate donors. S4S is proud to count literally hundreds of brands that are familiar to people around the world as supporters, among them adidas, Allbirds, Bombas, Brooks, Caleres, Crocs, DSW, HOKA, New Balance, Nike, The North Face, Timberland, Uggs, Under Armour, Vans, and Zappos.

TURNAROUND

By the time *Shoestrings* came out in 2018, we'd pulled out of the tailspin. We listened to smart, experienced people. We took careful notes on what worked and what didn't as we tried new strategies. Not only were we fully transparent about how and why entrepreneurs selling shoes worked; we also found that this openness forced us to improve the process.

In 2019, we "rebranded" microenterprise as 4Opportunity and our disaster relief efforts as 4Relief. Changing the names of these programs was far more than simply altering their titles. We had spent years learning what was required to accomplish our mission and to maximize our impact, setting us on a path of realistic, intentional growth.

The transformation that led to 4Opportunity is best demonstrated through an example of an early success story—one captured in *Shoestrings*—that taught us so many foundational lessons that we continue to apply every day. It also illustrates how we use mission-focused social enterprises (we call them direct partners) as the means to get product to entrepreneurs. It is the story of Samuel Darguin and his time in Haiti. The founder and director of the Haitian American Caucus (HAC) in Haiti, Darguin left New York City for Port-au-

Prince to help rebuild the country of his parents' birth after the devastating earthquake of January 2010. The disaster killed up to 316,000 people. After the immediate impacts of the earthquake had been "stabilized," Darguin's hands-on leadership brought renewed energy to the development of Haitian communities through sustainable solutions to the cyclical poverty that has plagued the nation since it won its independence in 1804.

After talking with the communities about the issues affecting their families, HAC focused on quality, affordable primary education, professional development, economic empowerment opportunities, and improved public health. Its economic development efforts focused mainly on extending microloans to aspiring entrepreneurs. Yet, even when HAC began offering very-low-interest microloans, this did nothing to change the hit-or-miss nature of entrepreneurship itself. This was because many of the businesses begun by loan recipients—such as agriculture, food, and beauty products/services—had low margins. Compounding this was the fledgling entrepreneurs' lack of business skills or training, which increased the odds that their businesses would fail. Sam needed a solution that tipped the odds of a new business's success in the borrower's—and thereby HAC's—favor.

The answer, of course, was shoes.

Sam was reluctant to get involved. It took some persuasion for him to recognize that this was a real opportunity—for his clients *and* for HAC—to generate a new revenue stream. "It took me some time to adjust and to really understand the market in Haiti, and how to really have the most impact on the most clients," Sam told me. "After some trial and error, some mistakes, I think I finally got it … where I'm able to really fine-tune our model … to where the women that we are servicing can really go out and see a benefit from that to help their families."

"For the first couple of months," Sam continued, "we were certainly underestimating the potential of the shoe market ... to really understand, in a country that doesn't produce any shoes, the actual value of a pair of shoes—and what that does for the person that is selling it, for the person who's buying it, and the impact that it could have on the entire country." It also boosted HAC's impact. Because of this targeted investment, the organization had the funds to build another floor on its school, which allowed it to accept 250 kids a full year ahead of schedule. A year of education and a guarantee of at least one hot meal, five days a week, was a very big deal.

We continued to learn from Sam, and from other partners around the world. We still work with Sam, although HAC efforts are now coordinated out of the US and the Dominican Republic because the area around Port-au-Prince is simply too dangerous. However, HAC is still providing shoes to more than 250 women entrepreneurs across the country. Sam has also brought the 4Opportunity model to the Dominican Republic, creating economic opportunity for Haitians who are often shut out of the Dominican system. There is a lot more that should be said about what Sam is doing, but the circumstances in which he operates also offer a good reminder about how tenuous and difficult our mission is because of where we work. If it were easy, S4S wouldn't need to be there. It is also a humbling reminder that our partners and the people they serve do the hardest work and take the greatest risks. Investing in them seems like the highest-return bet imaginable, by comparison. Supporting 4Opportunity with the help of organizations such as HAC isn't all we do, but it has been central to maximizing our impact.

ANOTHER VOICE | **Bernadette Lane**

Bernadette Lane retired as principal and managing director at CCS Fundraising, which provides fundraising, development services, and strategic consulting to clients in all sectors of the nonprofit community. Bernadette is personally committed to and experienced at working in low-income countries with a focus on lifting people out of poverty. She is an emeritus board chair for Soles4Souls.

Balance Beam

When I first joined the Soles4Souls board in 2013, they were in a "hair on fire" moment. There was lots of work to do and few board members to do it. The board members had little hands-on experience of what the organization was doing. They'd never been to Haiti or anywhere else where the social enterprise program was based, which made it difficult for them to communicate the organizational mission with others and garner support. One of the first things I did was to go to Haiti. Even before meeting the entrepreneurs, just seeing the marketplace, which in those days was little more than street vendors selling shoes from blankets set out in the dust among masses of people, brought home how severe the need was. Hearing some of the entrepreneurs talk about the transformative difference of having extra income from selling shoes cemented my understanding that this work was making such a difference in people's lives. By 2015, the board made the decision to go to Haiti, where we had our first-ever board meeting outside the US.

Even while still in Haiti on that first visit, Buddy, David Graben [COO], and I began having conversations about the social enterprise model and its impact. We asked ourselves whether it was important to focus on Haiti or expand to other places. Were we trying to go a mile wide and an inch deep or go a mile down and an inch wide? I thought we needed to greatly expand. But I also knew we didn't have enough product to expand meaningfully. We had to form a plan that would get more people interested in hosting shoe drives and get the footwear industry more committed to donating product. Most importantly, we had to get the story out. Having spent my career guiding nonprofits with fundraising, including putting boots on the ground to assist them, I knew that Soles4Souls had to learn not to be afraid of asking others to join them.

There were other things Soles4Souls had to improve as well, including doing a better job of learning their limitations and understanding the core nature of the places they served. From the beginning, I was impressed not only by their passion and their ability to use that to drive the mission forward but also by the leadership that allowed them to be nimble. They are a risk-taking organization, which is valuable, even if there were times when, as a board, we had to help them walk the balance beam between taking too much risk and its natural presence in entrepreneurial thinking. No worthy missions can be accomplished without some degree of measured risk, adaptability, and passion. When I think about organizations I've worked with, those that have an enormous drive and vision combined with passion are the ones that are the most successful. I shared such passion as I first stood in a Haitian marketplace and watched the tenacity of spirit I saw there.

NO PAIN, NO GAIN

You might have noticed that, when discussing his initial involvement with S4S, Sam shared that it took some "trial and error" and involved learning from "mistakes." This has been equally true for us.

We've done a good deal of thoughtful trial and error and made our share of mistakes. The question is, of course, did we learn from them? Throughout the book, I'll share some mistakes we made, the context for why the decisions that led to them proved to be wrong (something not always immediately evident), and, most importantly, the lessons we learned as illustrations that might spark your own reflection and problem-solving. Let me start by telling you a story that still keeps me humble almost seven years later.

Before I take you to Sierra Leone, a few words about how far we'd come between 2012 and 2018. Because poverty is so dire and so omnipresent in much of Africa, it was always a place we wanted to work. While we were trying to figure out how to do that in 2014, we were also on the hunt for new board members. We knew we needed experienced, credible people, so we began inviting (begging is such an ugly word!) new board members to help us envision a new future. We were fortunate early on to have Bernadette Lane join our board, and she agreed to serve as our board chair, the first to tackle that responsibility after Paul and Nelson Wilson, the two brothers who helped found S4S. Bernadette spent her entire professional career at CCS Fundraising, where she provided development services and strategic consulting to clients in all sectors of the nonprofit community. She also had vast volunteer and board experience working with international nonprofit organizations, including the Lions Club International Foundation and Rotary International in Africa. Bernadette is refreshingly direct, and as we discussed expansion into Africa, where we thought we were uniquely positioned to tackle the scourge of jiggers, a parasitic infection caused by insects, she didn't mince words when she told us that we had little idea what we were talking about. Jiggers is almost totally preventable by wearing shoes, and while it's rarely fatal, it's debilitating and painful, and in some cultures there's a lot of shame associated with having the disease. Bernadette emphasized that we were so eager to help that we had failed to consider how we would measure the impact of our work, the unique circumstances of our partners on the ground, the full scale of the health impacts, and the ecosystems (government, NGOs, community leaders, etc.) it takes to address an issue such as jiggers. And that's not even counting the enormous challenges that accompanied getting product into many African nations and through their customs systems. We not only desperately needed the right partners; we also would have to follow their lead and think in new patterns specific to the places and cultures they occupied. We had already sent one container of shoes to Kenya. It never made it past customs. We canceled the next shipment before we dug a deeper hole. Lesson learned.

The kind of expert guidance that people such as Bernadette provided allowed us to be far better partners, in part by recognizing what our capabilities and value really were. While not the only example of how board members played a key role in reshaping S4S, it's an excellent one. We could have made decisions that would have really put the organization at risk. Instead, we listened to the expertise we had access to, even though it felt as though we were backing down. Bernadette was right, but that tension between aspiration and execution has never gone away, and I hope it never does!

In part because of such sage advice, within a few years those downward metrics of 2012 were pointing the right way again. We had a sense of how to create long-term financial health. Stability gave us the confidence to ask ourselves, "What are we really aiming for?" While it's difficult to maintain our financial health in a world in which there is always tragedy, our finances steadily improved to the point where we could take on new challenges and realistically imagine extending our model in new places.

In fact, in 2017, over the course of several months, our COO David Graben and I figured out that, by 2030, S4S could reach an economic impact target of $1 billion. It felt like a slightly insane number (in lots of business books and circles it's called a BHAG, or Big Hairy Audacious Goal), but we didn't pull that number out of thin air. You'll hear the term BHAG with some regularity in this book because we were able to quantify our goal into a metric that became our north star—the guiding principle that provides us with a long-term vision and purpose. David and I had spent a lot of time in open-air markets on three continents, understanding prices and what product moved and what didn't. While it was more intuitive than quantitative, when we had the numbers evaluated by an expert consulting team in 2021, we were within a few dollars of the number for each pair of shoes and piece of clothing and had *underestimated* our economic impact! Eight years in, we remain on pace to hit the billion-dollar target.

At the time, we didn't know how we were going to get there, but we had the confidence, as an organization, to know that we could figure it out. What went into that target number turned out to be incredibly important in making decisions every day. Like a lot of what we do, such a decision was a simultaneous demonstration of genuine confidence and "Are you nuts?"

Sometimes, the lessons we had to learn—or relearn, as was often the case—would tip us to the "nutty" side, as our experience in Sierra Leone would show.

CHAPTER 2

Surviving Self-Inflicted Wounds and Unforeseen Loss

While COVID-19 definitely slowed progress in reducing global poverty, generally speaking, millions of people moved out of extreme poverty in places such as India, China, and South America in the last twenty-five years. In 2024, most international organizations agreed that the standard for measuring extreme poverty stood at less than $2.15 per day, up only slightly from just under $2.00 a day in 2017. The only place in the world where extreme poverty was worsening was Sub-Saharan Africa.

David and I shared the same attitude: If Sub-Saharan Africa was where the need was the greatest, then S4S needed to be there. And we needed money to develop a partnership there. It was no accident that one of the first big financial donations we received in support of an African presence came from the family foundation of one of my best friends—Milledge Hart. Milledge and Patti Hart were incredibly supportive of our entrepreneurial model and agreed with our hypothesis that S4S needed to expand into Africa. We didn't have a specific country or partner identified, but, thanks to them, we had some risk capital and a little momentum. One of my mantras over the years has been (and still is), "Clear on why; flexible on how." We knew our model had worked well elsewhere. The need to be in Africa was evident. Some seed funding, a little overconfidence, and not enough information … what could go wrong?

Perhaps a year or so before David and I developed our billion-dollar impact target, he received a call from a contact who told him that his father was living in Sierra Leone and working with the local people to improve cassava production rates (cassava is a common food crop, with a similar nutritional value to potatoes, that is also used as a starch, as bioethanol, in animal feed, and in a variety of products). David's contact had told his father about 4Opportunity, and the father, John, was all in. We were so excited about the chance to work in Africa that we didn't do sufficient homework. John had a team, money, and enthusiasm, and he was already on the ground working within a community, so we told ourselves, "We'll figure the rest out."

Sierra Leone is in West Africa, with a population of about 7 million. From 1991 to 2002, the country went through a brutal civil war that killed 50,000–70,000 people and displaced more than 2.5 million. Then, from 2014 to 2016, the country suffered a devastating outbreak of the Ebola virus that killed several thousand and terrified the nation. Without even getting into the dark chapters of colonial history and slavery, this was a place that knew more than most about heartache and poverty.

In 2016, David and I flew to Sierra Leone to meet John and his son. The work John was doing was real enough, and while extremely rudimentary and hardly the "factory" his son had described, he had mechanized some of the cassava root production. He had a team around him. Everyone was hustling. We met many of his workers, and they clearly respected him. John was saying all the right things, and there was no denying that he cared about helping the people around him. We got caught up in the moment and ignored the warning signs. John didn't have the cultural and economic expertise our typical partners possessed. He was a white guy from Idaho living in a village in the middle of a very underdeveloped country, and he didn't speak the language or understand the culture. Over lunch on the second day, it was clear that John's son was more interested in making money than helping local entrepreneurs, and the two almost immediately got into an argument that ended with the son—our contact—leaving the country on the next flight out.

Despite the red flags—looking back, they were really flashing red sirens—we sent John a shipping container of shoes. And miracle of miracles, it worked. Just like the model is supposed to. "Wonderful," we thought. "We've got a toehold in Sub-Saharan Africa and a chance to make a difference." We gave ourselves a big pat on the back. Go us.

Around the same time, a brand partner—a big donor— approached us and said, "We've got this problem. Maybe you could help us out." Without the okay from the partner, one of its factories in Asia had overproduced a run of shoes that the partner wasn't going to buy. The back and forth between a manufacturer and a brand is common, but this had been going on for several years. The factory was tired of storing the shoes, and the partner started seeing signs that the product was showing up in the gray market. The scale was substantial—tens of thousands of pairs. In approaching us, the company sought a way to solve its problem, help the factory save face, and do some good. That partner did an amazing job of bringing everyone together, but it provided a fairly small list of countries where the shoes could go. Most were in Africa. So we asked, "Is it okay if we send some of them to Sierra Leone?"

With the partner's approval, we sent a shipping container of really valuable shoes to John's warehouse in Freetown, Sierra Leone. Despite having a guard at the warehouse, someone stole the *entire* shipment.

John owed us approximately $150,000, and he had nothing to his name and no shoes to sell. No money. No product. $150,000 is a lot of money—full stop. At the time, however, it was a *shocking* amount of money to S4S. We flew back to Sierra Leone to see how we might salvage the enterprise. In a Hail Mary, we sent John more shoes in the hopes that selling them might help him to get out of the hole. The hole grew deeper. The loss broke John, and not just financially. His team disbanded in acrimony and blame. His health was so bad that he needed to leave Sierra Leone for a while. Just as we thought we were gaining some altitude, this felt like the beginning of another tailspin.

Shoestrings came out just a few months before this all unspooled. The book had been greeted with enthusiasm because there was a lot to celebrate! How, then, had we gotten it so wrong in Sierra Leone? We made fundamental mistakes. We moved too fast. We didn't do our homework. We fell prey to the "sunk cost fallacy" of throwing good money after bad. Honestly, they were different mistakes from those that had had S4S in a tailspin in 2012, but they were mistakes we should have known better than to make; the kind of mistakes experienced board members such as Bernadette Lane had taught us how to avoid. We ignored so much of what we had learned in building strong, patient partnerships with partners who knew about the unique cultural, political, and historical realities of each place we served. And we'd fallen into a trap that is common to organizations like ours that are sincerely driven by mission: Success can feel so good. I think that's a universal human reality. Yet, success—that sense of having made a difference in places where differences can determine whether a child goes to sleep hungry or goes to school, or whether a mother can put a roof over her family's head—can lead to a mistaken self-satisfaction. This is not unique to nonprofits. Plenty of for-profit companies breathe their own exhaust. But believing that you really are making a difference is a particular risk in the social sector because that's the mission. Soles4Souls was certainly not immune ... we made a difference; just not the right kind.

In Sierra Leone, we did so many things wrong that we would never do now. I'm certain we'll make other mistakes, but they won't be the same ones. That's one important lesson we have acquired on our journey: Just as there will be new problems to encounter, we will make new mistakes. It *is* worth celebrating surviving a crisis, but the learning that accompanies survival does not end. I take ownership of what we got wrong in Sierra Leone. As we expanded to Guatemala, the Philippines, Belize, and Chile, the painful lessons we learned dramatically changed our approach to evaluating partners and places. A few years in, we have seen a much better success rate. We're even beginning to explore how we find the right opportunity to try again in Africa!

FAILURE ALWAYS FEELS PERSONAL

About that $150,000 we lost in Sierra Leone ... as a nonprofit, the simple reality is that a mistake that costs real dollars often necessarily means that we have lost someone else's money, which hurts a lot more. While the mistakes we made created a *significant* financial loss, because many of our successful lessons had become ingrained in how we operated, it was not a *catastrophic* loss. We screwed up, but we could recover. And we could examine the mistakes we made and avoid them in the future. I knew we could learn from the experience even as it was happening, but that's small consolation when you feel you have failed. It certainly did not remove the sting of having to explain to others who had contributed to this new venture that we'd gotten it wrong.

In this case, we would never have made it into Africa at all were it not for that sizable donation from the Hart Family Foundation, its first investment in the Soles4Souls mission. To make matters worse, Milledge Hart is one of my closest friends. I have known him since 1991. Milledge possesses one of the finest business minds I have ever encountered, has vast experience in diverse fields from investment banking to HVAC, and is someone I have turned to for advice time and time again. Calling Milledge and Patti and telling them that we had lost their donation was every bit as difficult as departing Sierra Leone with the knowledge that we had let down so many people who had such desperate need. It wasn't a call I ever wanted to make to any donor who had staked their belief in our mission, but breaking such news to friends was awful. It is so much easier when transparency is saying "the guys before us made a mess and we're fixing it," but when it's your mess and your friends and you took their money, that truly tests your integrity. Transparency is only a word until it costs you something. The sense of failure I experienced felt very personal.

Experienced and classy, Milledge and Patti, to their credit, didn't let us off the hook, but they didn't condemn us or walk away either. Instead, they asked, "What happened? Why did it go wrong? You didn't get the result you expected, so what did you learn?" Their generosity of understanding was remarkable. Perhaps more remarkable was their willingness to become more involved in the S4S mission when they could have told us that they didn't want to waste their time. Not too long after confessing to them what had happened in Sierra Leone, I vividly remember being out for a run in our local park when my phone rang. It was Patti. Somewhere in our conversation she essentially asked, "When are you going to ask Milledge to be on the board?"

My response was, "Never. I want to maintain our friendship more than I want him to be on our board."

Patti replied, "Those things are not mutually exclusive." A true "duh" moment for me.

Milledge not only joined the board; he eventually became our chair. He and the other board members became deeply involved with the guidance and expertise a nonprofit organization needs to be successful. It was little surprise, then, that despite reaching the end of his two-year term as board chair in June of 2020, while we were in the thick of COVID-19 and the world seemed to be falling apart, the rest of the board members asked him if he would stay on for one more year. They, and we, knew his leadership would be immeasurable as we developed our response to sustaining the organization during the pandemic.

ANOTHER VOICE | **Milledge Hart**

After a successful career as an operating executive, Milledge Hart now guides multiple organizations as a board member and advisor. He serves as chair of both the global investment bank Drake Star Partners and Quarles Petroleum. In addition, he is deeply engaged in impact investing initiatives, including the Hart Family Foundation, which he cofounded with his wife. He is an emeritus Soles4Souls board chair.

Discovering Discipline

My connection to Soles4Souls began through my long-standing friendship with Buddy. Like him, I have always recognized poverty as one of the world's most pressing issues. I was immediately drawn to Soles4Souls' innovative approach to reducing poverty through social enterprise. Learning that 80% of all clothes end up in landfills—a staggering and troubling statistic—I admired how the organization tackled this issue while empowering individuals, especially women, to establish businesses in developing countries. I believed in the potential for real, meaningful change and was eager to contribute. In fact, I had quietly hoped Buddy might ask me to join the board.

When that opportunity came, I didn't hesitate. However, I was fully aware of the significant challenges the organization faced. Achieving financial stability depended on many factors aligning successfully. While I recognized Soles4Souls' potential to drive revenue growth and amplify impact, the scale of that opportunity was uncertain. What I did know was that the organization's mission was inspiring and that the board was comprised of fascinating individuals. Yet, surprisingly, fundraising was not an expectation for board members. For a nonprofit focused on eradicating poverty, this struck me as an untapped opportunity. Changing this culture took time and effort, but it was a critical shift. It allowed the board to align with the organization's biggest transformation: the way Buddy and his leadership team began to run the nonprofit with the discipline and rigor of a business.

This discipline has been transformative, although it wasn't always part of Soles4Souls' DNA. I saw its absence firsthand during an ill-fated partnership in Sierra Leone. Although the partner was capable, it wasn't the right fit, and the venture resulted in significant financial losses. For my wife Patti and me, however, these losses represented a speed bump—a tough lesson but also an opportunity for growth. As with any setback, there's value in learning, and Soles4Souls embraced that philosophy.

The organization's ability to adapt and strengthen is a testament to its culture of transparency and accountability. This culture stems in part from the collaborative and honest dynamic between Buddy and his board. We prioritized creating space for candid discussions. At the end of every board meeting, we would excuse Buddy and the management team, allowing the board members to voice their ideas, thoughts, or concerns freely. Later, Buddy and I would debrief, addressing both the positive and the challenging feedback. His willingness to listen and act—even when reluctant—has been a hallmark of his leadership and has deeply influenced the organization.

Today, that same transparency is embedded across Soles-4Souls, fostering integrity and resilience. Transparency is one of the qualities that first drew me to Buddy—his ability to speak plainly, without pretense or games. Seeing those traits reflected throughout Soles4Souls has been inspiring. The organization has not only grown in impact but has done so in a way that ensures every step is measured, disciplined, and meaningful. That evolution is what keeps me so invested in its mission and its future.

FROM SELF-INFLICTED WOUNDS TO UNFORESEEABLE DISASTERS

While the debacle that was Sierra Leone was largely avoidable, some of the biggest challenges come out of nowhere. A universal example we can all relate to is the arrival of a global pandemic. And indeed, COVID-19 was challenging given the very nature of the work S4S does. When the pandemic hit, we were right back at the "flexible on how" part of my mantra, and while I was uncertain how we would sustain our operations, I believed we had the "muscle memory" to figure it out because of the team we had built. I didn't know exactly how we would get through COVID-19, but I never doubted that we would.

But the biggest 2020 disaster we faced was not COVID-19; it was the loss of David Graben. David was one of the first employees at S4S. He had seen it through every spin of the wheel. He was an incredible operator and an encyclopedia of institutional knowledge.

He served as our COO and later as our president. In 2012, when the CEO position became vacant, he was the interim CEO, and he wanted the job. The board hired me. So needless to say, ours was not a ready-made partnership. We were not immediate friends. But then we traveled around the world together for eight years. We were shoulder to shoulder through every step of the organization's recovery. We often disagreed, but we always worked through it. The relationship that developed between us over those eight years was one of the most amazing of my life.

In 2018, about the time we were able to see that S4S was really on a growth track, David was diagnosed with cancer. In typical David fashion, he set out to kick cancer's butt. It was a hellish few months for him and his family, but later that year, doctors told David his cancer was in remission. The entire organization celebrated. We were all shocked, then, when David announced in late January of 2020 that the cancer was back, and he returned to chemo. We were even more shocked that, this time around, something about David seemed different, less defiant.

In early February 2020, *The Tennessean* published an article that essentially said, "Soles4Souls is back. You can trust these guys. We're glad they are part of our community." It felt like redemption, but it was muted by our worry about David's health. In March, COVID-19 hit. I remember thinking in the early weeks of the pandemic that there was no way we were going to navigate all the complexities it would bring without David, yet we had to find a way because he was in the midst of his cancer battle. I spent time thinking about what David would do if the tables were turned and came away knowing that we had to find a way to adapt to the COVID-19 world with or without him. He would find a way to separate grief from solving the problems of the business. I've been reading the *Daily Stoic* for many years, and I kept coming back to a quotation from Epictetus, one of the earliest Stoics: "Man is not worried by real problems so much as by his imagined anxieties about real problems." This really brought me clarity. I realized that we could not skimp on the emotion we felt at the thought of losing David, *and* that our emotion could not allow us to avoid the work that needed done.

In May, David lost his battle, and we lost him. I still miss him every day.

FINDING DIRECTION IN LOSS

It won't surprise you that when trying to figure out how to move S4S forward after David's death, one of the people I consistently turned to for advice was Milledge Hart. He and David had been close as well, and he felt David's loss keenly. Perhaps because of Milledge's deep, diverse experience, and perhaps because he had more distance from the situation than I did, Milledge was able, gently, to help me see that the changes required of S4S in David's absence presented an opportunity. I doubt I'll ever have the kind of work partnership I shared with David again in my professional life. Because David had been with S4S from so early in its history, and because he was a terrific operator, much of his world view, like his experience, was different from mine. We had succeeded in turning those differences into strengths. Now, in his absence, we needed to be ready to embrace new differences and new directions.

Milledge is not a "hide the ball" kind of guy. We have developed the kind of trusting friendship and communicative working partnership in which he could give me the hard advice that any leader needs to hear with regularity. At one point, Milledge said to me, "I know you love the turnaround story. I get it. But it's time you let it go. It's time to move on." He was right. I'm proud of what we've accomplished, and the next chapter shares some of those accomplishments, but it was high time I let go of the past enough to focus on the future.

Looking back, I can now see that our need to adapt—to David's death, to COVID-19—forced S4S to become a more resilient organization. We see the benefits of that every day. It has allowed us to take on new challenges, move into new places around the globe, develop new programs, and form new partnerships.

What united David and me, what attracted us to S4S in the first place, was its mission. We had discovered a cause we believed in and a model that demonstrated results. Keeping both in mind, particularly the economic impact lens David and I created, the losses that marked 2020, ultimately, created a stronger, more flexible, more confident organization.

CHAPTER 3

Strategy and Results

The abilities to be resilient and adaptable were at the core of what helped us survive 2020, just as they had been key to success in the first three or four years following 2012. To resilience and adaptability, I'll add collaboration as a central tenet for what allowed us to move from crisis to success. I see eight key strategies that allowed us to complete a turnaround; they form the framework of several of the chapters that follow:

- establishing core values
- clarifying mission and setting a vision
- implementing a robust operating system
- building a strong team
- engaging a committed board
- developing strategic partnerships that fuel growth
- powering change and growth
- identifying and activating a north star

In 2012, because the tailspin had multiple causes, everything had to be addressed—*stat*. We could not afford to work on one problem at a time, nor was there ever a single solution. Everything was interconnected. For example, we simply could not form partnerships with organizations that reflected our core values if we had not identified what they were or made certain that we applied them consistently in our own team.

But, before I get to core values in the next chapter, I want to give you a sense of how these strategies worked. There's a reason this book is not just about the tailspin!

Remember that $1 billion in economic impact by 2030 target? As of the end of 2024, we have generated more than $698 million in economic impact. Through our 4Opportunity program alone, in 2024, we provided 4,842,102 pairs of new and gently used shoes and 2,491,353 articles of clothing. Entrepreneurs who sell goods because of the 4Opportunity program have increased their household incomes by more than 200%—more than five times the international poverty line of $2.15 per person per day.[1] While our annual revenue initially dipped from the $4 million recorded in 2012 as we confronted the causes of our crisis, we have almost quintupled that figure with about the same number of employees as we had twelve years ago.

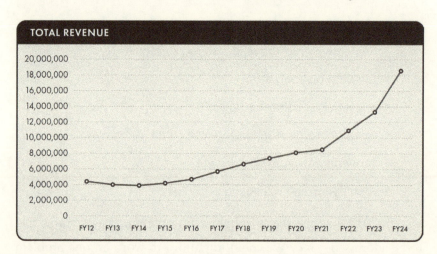

---

[1] "Fact Sheet: An Adjustment to Global Poverty Lines," World Bank Group, last updated September 14, 2022, https://www.worldbank.org/en/news/factsheet/2022/05/02/fact-sheet-an-adjustment-to-global-poverty-lines.

STRATEGY AND RESULTS

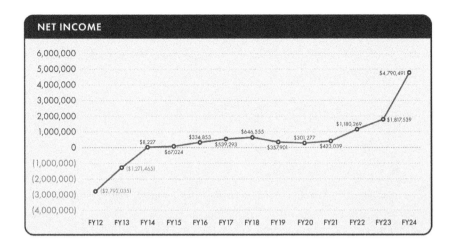

We've grown in the countries we previously served and have expanded into new ones. And we have been able to increase our impact by creating a new domestic program called 4EveryKid. Launched in 2020, we partner with schools across the US to get new, branded athletic shoes to children who are experiencing homelessness, eliminating a barrier to educational and extracurricular opportunities. By the end of the 2024–25 school year, more than 525,000 students will have received new shoes and socks, contributing to their social, physical, and emotional health.

These are just some of the metrics that offer evidence that we are succeeding in work that matters. We have played a part in transforming lives. And we have transformed ourselves in the process.

 ANOTHER VOICE | **Raul Carrasco**

Raul Carrasco is the founder and CEO of World Compass Foundation (WCF), which has a mission to drive sustainable change by shaping leaders and investing in impactful businesses, people, and ideas. Based in Honduras, WCF develops entrepreneurs through business school training, active learning, and job creation. A former Brazilian jujitsu

champion, Raul is also the founder of Souldiers, a values-based program that uses the martial arts as a transformative tool for youth empowerment. He is one of Soles4Souls' longest-serving direct partners.

Changing Mindsets

Fifteen years ago, when I started WCF and first partnered with Soles4Souls, I was a thirsty guy, wanting to create impact, support the community, create legacy ... all that romantic stuff of trying to be the superhero and save the world. I still have that passion, but I've evolved. So has Soles4Souls. We have both grown up.

When we started working together, S4S used the term "microentrepreneurs." What I have learned is that I don't want to be "micro" anything. I want to make a big impact. My basic instinct has always been to question everything: Don't talk to me; show me the facts. I'm not interested in marketing; I want evidence of change. Looking for the facts has taught me that charity accomplishes nothing. Charity is people showing up one time, giving something, and never coming back. People must grow. We are in a war against poverty. If people are simply given things, they get hurt in the end because that kind of charity creates dependency. They don't need a superhero; they need role models and teachers who understand business. They must learn how to fight for themselves.

In the early years of WCF, over a hundred charitable organizations came to my city, El Progreso. Today, only two remain. Soles4Souls is one of them. We are symbiotic partners. We want to create sustainability for my customers. That takes a partner that stays, just as Soles4Souls has done, because you need to attack the mentality of the people. They have grown up thinking small; thinking like people who live in poverty. Opportunity matters, but what matters even more is mindset. If we really want to save the world, success comes 10% from providing opportunity and 90% from challenging mindset. If you change that percentage in somebody, then you're going to be able to see a new leader grow, a new entrepreneur with a totally different kind of life from the one they had before. If you can do that to somebody's mind, then you are really breaking the cycle of poverty. Then, you have to replicate that over and over. Soles4Souls provides opportunity, but even more importantly, it gives me the room to innovate, to take this passion I feel in my heart and attack poverty with the mindset of a Navy Seal focused on their mission.

SEIZING OPPORTUNITY

Statistics tell part of the story. People tell it more fully. Like Kimberly Vasquez, whom I first met on a 2019 trip to Honduras where I spent considerable time with S4S's longtime partner Raul Carrasco. Based in El Progreso, Raul, with S4S's help, started as a microenterprise partner in 2014 through his organization WCF, supplying shoes to individual entrepreneurs, mostly women, helping them disrupt the cycle of poverty. Raul could be the poster child for *From Tailspin to Tailwind* because his transitional arc is nearly identical to ours, evolving from a passionate, entrepreneurial-spirited fighter with more street smarts than business experience. In *Shoestrings*, Tiffany Turner, a longtime S4S travel leader who is now spearheading our 4EveryKid program, aptly described Raul this way: "Raul is a mixed martial arts [MMA] champion! He also enjoys painting and is learning the violin. That's just the start of his many contrasting sides. Across his chest, he carries a gun and a machete (named "Mona Lisa"). But he also loves to sing a Celine Dion song, karaoke-style. Raul is a teacher, a leader, and very much a fighter!"

"Fighter" is a good descriptor for Kimberly as well. She runs the warehouse for WCF, which serves both small and medium-sized entrepreneurs and provides inventory for three retail locations. She's from El Reso—a desperate place with few opportunities, particularly for a single mom. She once tried to escape Honduras with her two kids, paying gangs and coyotes to get to Mexico, where she, like a lot of refugees fleeing poverty, ended up in a Mexican jail. She was injured while she was being held, and then she was deported, arriving home broke and out of options. Today an international jujitsu and MMA competitor, she first met Raul through combat sports. Raul saw something in her and gave her a job. Now she's in charge of production for Raul's steadily growing organization, freeing him from his warehouse, which has allowed him to expand his retail channel and spend more time helping entrepreneurs. When I last saw Kimberly in August 2024, she was about to travel to Brazil for an MMA match. She's bought a car. She's saving for a house. Her children's lives have been completely transformed. The confidence she has in herself to make a difference and be a role model for her family and community is every bit as inspiring as any S4S story I could share.

Kimberly's is one story of thousands. It represents exactly why I believed S4S had a chance of a fresh life in 2012. It demonstrates why we think our audacious billion-dollar impact target is worth embracing. More importantly, it represents why we believe that target is entirely achievable.

I ended *Shoestrings* in 2018 with a call to action for readers to join our cause. That invitation remains open, of course, but with *From Tailspin to Tailwind* I want to dig into *how* we transformed S4S into an organization that can consistently help provide life-changing opportunities for people like Kimberly; an organization that can make Nicole's nana proud. We got there by learning from our mistakes, by becoming transparent about who we are and what we do, by acting entrepreneurially, and by holding ourselves accountable for results, embracing adaptability, and practicing resiliency.

Your organization probably looks different from ours. Your objectives are unique. The characteristics of your crisis are likely distinct. But if you want to take a strategic approach to surviving crisis—either one already playing out or the possibility of one on the horizon—you don't have a chance if you haven't defined, and learned to live by, shared core values. That's where we go next.

CHAPTER 4

Core Values = Culture

The culture of any organization is shaped by the worst behavior the leader is willing to tolerate.
—SCHOOL CULTURE REWIRED,
BY STEVE GRUENERT AND TODD WHITAKER

As I have shared, the problems Soles4Souls faced in 2010 when *The Tennessean* began publishing its series of articles were myriad, and nearly all were of the organization's own making. Those articles preceded me, so some of what I know from that time I've pieced together and some comes from what others have shared. But my sense remains that those making the big decisions worsened the situation in two ways: 1) most of the employees were left in the dark, and 2) the leadership dismissed the reporter, Bob Smietana, as a sensationalist looking to unearth a "there" that wasn't there. Bob is a skilled investigative journalist, and while his official beat for the paper was religion, he understood social enterprise. He has strong instincts and is not a "gotcha" kind of reporter. The S4S leadership reaction was textbook 100% wrong. They put on the website, "We're suing *The Tennessean* for defamation." As Mark Twain is supposed to have said, "Never get in a fight with anyone who buys ink by the barrel." It was like increasing airspeed while in a tailspin. S4S's reaction seemingly revealed that its leadership had no core values to turn to in a time of crisis.

WHAT NEEDED TO CHANGE

Actually, that's not true. Another way to think about it is that values = culture. And as Seth Godin says, "Culture is the way we do things around here." Just because values aren't written down doesn't mean that people don't know "how we do things around here." The values we don't acknowledge are just as powerful as the ones we do. When it came to decision-making, the organizational culture I stepped into at S4S in 2012 seemed to value behaviors such as "stay in your lane," "bigger is better," and "story matters more than facts." This led to a narrow understanding of responsibilities, little collaboration, and a lot of passing the buck. There were frequent miscommunications because people got dinged if they strayed outside the lines. They weren't incentivized to think about the wider organization or how various roles fit together, and oddly, in an organization that was losing revenue, a great deal of emphasis was placed on achieving individual benchmarks that triggered bonuses, no matter how the organization performed.

The "stay in your lane" mentality helps explain why so many people within the organization were caught off guard when *The Tennessean* began reporting on business practices more of them should have been aware of. There was a pervasive attitude that employees didn't get paid to help each other, which is ironic in an organization rooted in philanthropy. These traits created a culture that was competitive but lacked accountability; a dangerous combination. There were values in place, of course, but the dominant culture actually accelerated the tailspin. It also explains why nothing that Smietana "unearthed" was inaccurate. His reporting showed that S4S was on the wrong track, and that those at the top, making the decisions, had charted a course for its downfall.

My first few months were focused primarily on two things: coming to understand the depth and breadth of the problems we faced, and stopping the immediate financial hemorrhaging and reputational battering. I asked Les Ward, with whom I had worked at the Young Presidents' Organization (YPO), to help assess the situation. In just a few weeks, he came back with the news that things were far worse than we had thought. The losses were deeper, there was little cash available, we were out of covenant with our bank, and a lawsuit that had been going on for years was bleeding S4S dry. Shortly after that, in an act of friendship and bravery, Les agreed to be our CFO. He, David, and I knew we had to move quickly, so we set to work with the bankers and lawyers and made the decisions that would keep the lights on. It wasn't easy, but it was the kind of thing we could throw ourselves into because there were tangible needs that required tangible actions, right now.

By 2014, although there were still plenty of financial problems to address, we reached a point where we could focus on the underlying decisions and behaviors that had contributed to the tailspin, including those that had almost bankrupted the organization. Les took the lead on sorting out the finances, settled the lawsuit for pennies on the dollar, and even found a new bank (which is a story in itself!). He was exactly what we needed.

David stepped up in profoundly important ways. Working with our indirect (for-profit) partners, he was often able to get them to pay for product in advance of our being able to ship it. On one hand, it was a very good business decision because we were able to use them like a line of credit when we were unable to get one from our bank. On the other hand, this was only possible because David put his and our reputations on the line. Those partners took substantial risks trusting S4S, which was no small feat when there was so much bad press. Because of the hard work on the financial front, we had more bandwidth for other aspects of the organization's needs and began to focus on shifting the values to the ones we aspired to.

As we tried to define who we wanted to be, I thought it was important to remove some of the hierarchy and create an environment in which we could talk honestly with each other. By late 2012, we started a weekly all-hands meeting—we were small enough then that everyone except our Alabama warehouse team could fit in the Nashville conference room! We each shared the most important thing we were working on. This created a lot more awareness of what was going on. It also allowed us to recognize wins—and we needed every opportunity we could find to celebrate! Twelve years on, we still have our weekly "Monday Morning Meeting," so it's a part of our culture.

This was an organic way to begin the process, capitalizing on opportunities where we could sit down with one another and have conversations. While there certainly were sessions when we gathered people in a room with a whiteboard and Post-it notes, we didn't approach the values-defining process by forming a committee. Most of the decisions about culture emerged from the context of problem-solving in specific, real-time circumstances and then stopping to talk about the positive things that occurred once we reached solutions.

SOLES4SOULS' CORE VALUES

- **Transparent:** We tell the truth to ourselves, each other, and everyone else. That goes for everything from financials to programs to team members. Bad news is okay because it's a chance to improve. Good news is welcome because it's a chance to celebrate.

- **Entrepreneurial:** If we're going to serve entrepreneurs, we need to act like entrepreneurs! We take calculated risks, learn from failure, and act like an owner. We are results-focused, but always through the lens of our mission and north star.

CORE VALUES = CULTURE

- **Accountable:** We deliver on our promises to each other and those we serve. Words matter, and if we say we're going to do something, we do it. If we can't, we own it without making excuses and don't surprise others who are affected.

- **Meaningful:** The work we do matters to us at Soles4Souls *and* to those we serve. S4S is more than a job; it's an opportunity to make a difference in the world. Every team member should feel connected to that work, but our work isn't truly meaningful unless those who buy/receive/donate shoes and clothes or donate money to support our mission believe it matters, too.

IT STARTS WITH HONESTY

My one nonnegotiable was transparency. But I didn't start by articulating transparency as a value. I didn't have to. All I had to do was remind us how we arrived at a crisis. On more than one occasion, I said, "Folks, we must earn everyone's trust again. We're in the hole, but we can regain trust by being honest about what happened, where we are, and where we're going." Mutual awareness allowed us to have conversations about why that was true. We asked one another the hard questions, such as, "Who is buying these shoes? Where do they end up? Why has it proven so difficult to track the finances?" With honest questions and honest answers, we were able to form the framework to ask the larger question: "Who do we want to be?"

Transparency started with one of the things that had been most hidden: our fiscal health. My experience is that, often, people say they want transparency but aren't ready for the bad news that might show up. Full transparency scared many on the S4S team, and with good reason. There were more than a few months when making payroll meant not submitting executive team expenses, holding off on paying some bills (though we always paid eventually!), or working hard to get out one more load of shoes. Once we had financials we could trust, we started every month by opening the books so everyone could see exactly where we stood. Some thrived on jumping over every hurdle. Others left because they didn't think it was worth it or, worse, that we were going to fail. Some days, they seemed like the smart ones. But those who believed in S4S kept showing up and doing the hard work of translating our aspirations into action.

We took the same approach of transparency outside S4S. We received important guidance from Steve Silvers, a crisis communication consultant I had known for more than a decade, who reinforced what people in the footwear industry were telling us: Be candid. When partners or donors called and asked us about the newspaper articles, our response was to tell them what had happened and what we were doing about it. Their acceptance of our openness was far from immediate, but when they saw for themselves that our actions matched our words, bit by bit, they came around. Steve was quick to see an opportunity to change the public conversation about S4S when Bob Smietana approached us in 2014, wanting to do a follow-up piece. Bob had every reason to believe that he would be stonewalled and fed BS by the executive team. He came in like any good reporter, looking for facts (and probably expecting a fight). We drew out our business model on a whiteboard. We opened our books. We showed him exactly where the money went, why we were losing money, and how we planned to change our approach to social enterprise. I told Smietana, "Selling shoes this way is a great thing, not something to be embarrassed about. And here's why." The more he learned, the more he became intrigued by our business model. Ultimately, he wrote a fair piece that talked about our turnaround progress—not a full-throated endorsement, but a sign that we could be trusted. This was definitely a win.

For years, I spent a lot of time having difficult conversations. This included talking openly with everyone from our biggest corporate donors, our partners on the other side of the globe, and grandmothers in Tennessee to small businesses in Milwaukee. Two stories show how real those conversations were.

EARNING TRUST

I vividly recall the first time I met Jim Salzano, who at that time was running a footwear brand and was the board chair for the Two Ten Foundation, the footwear industry's charitable arm. He'd been in the footwear industry his whole life. Shortly after we were introduced, Jim said, "Hey, I know you're brand-new to this thing [I had been at S4S for less than a month], but you need to understand how deep the hole you're in is. You're going to have to spend a lot of time explaining to people what went wrong and what you're going to do about it. It's not going to be any fun, but it's the only way forward." While I was taken aback by Jim's bluntness, his comments reinforced my commitment to be truthful to ourselves and to others. Ultimately, I am incredibly grateful to Jim. It would have been easier for him to say nothing … he had no stake in S4S. But I know now that his advice came from somebody who cares about helping others and about the industry.

It was only a few months later that I got a call from another Jim—Jim Sadjak, the owner of Stan's Fit For Your Feet, a family business that's been selling shoes in and around Milwaukee since 1950. Jim had been collecting donated shoes in his stores for several years. He was one of the folks who felt betrayed. I flew to Milwaukee to meet him and his family (now, all four of Jim's children are running the company, but some were still in high school then), and, well, it sucked. Jim had put his reputation on the line. People trusted him and his family, and he needed me to recognize the negative impact on him and his business. He felt misled about where donated products went and expected us to come clean. I shared what I knew to be true at that time and promised to be transparent about our work in the future. There was little more that I could do in that moment, but hearing how personal and local S4S was for Jim offered another key step in understanding how and why our work mattered. It was rough getting chewed out. But we deserved it, and it helped start the healing.

I remain convinced that we could not have turned the organization around without transparency. It was so satisfying when Jim Salzano, who now runs Jones & Vining, one of the industry leaders in making shoe lasts (a mechanism used to define the shape, fit, and size of a shoe), told me recently that he thinks S4S has done an amazing job. He then asked me what his company could do to support our 4EveryKid program. To have someone so respected in the industry recognize how far we had come meant the world.

ANOTHER VOICE | **Michael Brown**

Michael Brown has been active with Soles4Souls since before it was officially called that, first volunteering for the organization during its response to Hurricane Katrina. He is vice president, Warehousing and Logistics at Soles4Souls.

The Culture of People

As a working team, we collaboratively established the core values of S4S, and these have continued to evolve over time. We keep them out front as a common thread through everything we do. The changes we have undergone in our culture, with the growth we have achieved and even the core values themselves, have been a product of the outstanding people who have come through our organization, past and present. The culture is a result of the staff, outstanding leadership, board members, volunteers, partners, and our strong commitment to both the mission and the people we serve, and to each other. They are present in all our decisions. A good illustration of this for me is the very fact that, as an organization, we have chosen Wadley, Alabama, for our warehouse facility, because it is a vital presence in the rural area where we're located and a source of pride for our team members here. Wadley is a place with few job opportunities and low economic diversity. To me, the choice to remain committed to Wadley reveals the S4S core values of being entrepreneurial and meaningful. It would have been so easy for the organization to move its warehouse so that it was closer to its headquarters in Nashville, or to a major transportation hub, but the S4S commitment to people and place is deeper than that.

The Wadley facility has grown and adapted to meet the needs of the organization admirably. But what I am proudest of, and what is one of the most meaningful parts of my work at S4S, is the people I have gotten to work with. We do a good job of measuring the impact we have for the people and places we serve with our programs, and we sometimes forget that S4S has had just as meaningful an impact on the lives of those of us who work here and on our community. I can provide statistics on the number of people we currently employ and the numbers who have worked here over the years; but to me, the best reflection of our core values can be found in other kinds of statistics, the kind that will not show up anywhere but that are special to me, such as the sixteen employees who have been children or foster children of other employees; those who have worked for us for more than a decade; or those who have attended school while working for us. Many of these people have moved on to become emergency responders, business owners, engineers, ministers, and teachers. Like our missions through 4Opportunity and 4EveryKid, S4S has provided opportunities—many times, moving people out of poverty—for those here at home.

S4S is a unique place that lives by its values. I or any member of my team know we can communicate with any member of the larger S4S team on any issue or with any questions. Team members at all levels of leadership include the operations staff in discussions and reach out for our input. It is the kind of organization where the CEO makes the day-long roundtrip from Nashville to Wadley several times a year because he values the chance to meet face-to-face. He's also the kind of person who, upon arriving at the warehouse, knows the name of every team member who works there. This engagement is an embodiment of our culture. The local cultures and daily routines in Nashville or Wadley or El Progreso may be very different, but the longer I have been in my position, the more I have grown to understand the many more ways we are alike.

TRANSPARENCY LEADS THE WAY TO OTHER VALUES

As a result of our many conversations about transparency, the obvious question was "What are our other values?" Had we not been transparent with everyone in the organization, I don't think this question would ever have been asked. As we identified the values we found indispensable, we had the good fortune that it was easy to remember them with the acronym TEAM: Transparent. Entrepreneurial.

Accountable. Meaningful. We got to TEAM because we focused on our "why." And we make sure we stay focused on this by always living our values. Inseparable from one another, the values are the foundational principles for any success we've had.

Once we got beyond the "Yep, we sell shoes as part of our mission. We're proud of that and here's why and how it works" phase of open conversations, we could deepen that by looking at the *E*: We could exponentially increase our impact by focusing on entrepreneurs. If we could not embrace an entrepreneurial mindset ourselves, we would never understand our partners well enough to serve them properly. The entrepreneurs on the ground lived in day-to-day realities that we could barely imagine in the US, in conditions that, while shocking and memorable when our team, volunteers, and board visited those places, were temporary for us. The demanding conditions—where poverty was ubiquitous and political unrest, violence, war, poor infrastructure, and difficult access to healthcare were common—required our entrepreneurial partners to be agile, adaptable, and creative. It's not too much of an exaggeration to say that being entrepreneurial was a matter of life and death for them.

We had to adopt that mindset. We need people who want to be part of something bigger; people who help teammates even when it takes them out of their comfort zone; people who solve problems, not those who only follow procedures or wait to be told what to do; people who are so dedicated to our mission that they're focused on how to accomplish objectives, no excuses. When a shipping container gets seized by customs in Moldova or a currency is devalued by 20% overnight, it takes creativity and adaptability to work out a solution, often with distant officials, distributors, or on-the-ground partners, and sometimes it means making rapid, complex decisions or rethinking our financial expectations.

Just as for-profit entrepreneurs learn that no two markets are identical, our model needed to be flexible. The precise logistics required to support a partner in Honduras are not the same as those required in Haiti, just as getting a load of shoes to Syria for disaster relief is different from getting a container of shoes and clothes to families affected by hurricanes in Florida.

ANOTHER VOICE | **Tiffany Turner**

Tiffany Turner is vice president of outreach at Soles4Souls. She leads the 4Relief and 4EveryKid programs.

Team

I started at Soles4Souls first as a volunteer, then as a part-time employee, and eventually, because I loved what they were doing, as a full-time team member in 2011. When I started leading what we now call our 4Relief program, we had about 430 partners. Most donations were based around disaster relief to nonprofits that served people in crisis, whether because of a natural disaster or because they were unhoused, or to support outreach such as afterschool programming. In those days, there wasn't always a clear communication process with our partners about how and where the shoes were distributed, which was something we had to remedy if we were going to grow. At our low point, if I hadn't believed in what we were doing, I would not have stayed. But I knew the end users we were serving. I knew the work we were doing, and I knew it was good. To date, we have served over two thousand nonprofit global partners. We know a lot about them and about the work they do. We have clear communications about their processes and where the donations go. Every day, I'm in contact with partners all around the world, making sure that brand-new products get to people in need.

I wasn't in a leadership position in the early days. Today, I am. This has given me a much wider perspective of S4S. Now, I sit in on board meetings and have seen how our cultural values—such as transparency, which is very much a real thing here—mean that what is discussed in those meetings is translated from the top down. There are no walls. I remember vividly after the first board meeting I attended how our CEO addressed the whole S4S team at the start of the fiscal year and was completely transparent about what the board had discussed.

It's a value that is embedded in our culture, just like entrepreneurship. Our teams know what we're doing in our world, but we're also open to asking, "How does this work? Is there another way to do this?" I remember I was once in a planning meeting for an event with one of our partners, who said, "Wow, you have this down." My coworker, a new employee, replied, "Well, she should, she does the same thing every day." After we left the meeting, I politely said, "Hey, we need to have a quick chat. I don't do the same thing every day. In theory, yes, but every event is different. Every partner is different. You have to understand the partner and the community and the culture. No two are alike, so no day is the same." This reality has created a great balance of people who are going to do everything to ensure they get the operations of what we do right and those who are visionaries and risk-takers.

These are all parts of our core values. We keep TEAM in front of us. I talk about our team values almost once a day with someone, either external or internal. About a year ago, one of our 4EveryKid partners completed a follow-up survey, and on their own they listed all the words of TEAM in their response. I remember thinking, *This is crazy*, but my next thought was that it totally made sense. It takes all of our values to reach the M in TEAM—meaning-

> ful. What we do is human-centered work. Every pair of shoes we distribute ends with a human being. Every one of their situations is different. Everyone has a story. Our work is meaningful because, for the people we serve, it's meaningful to them.

There is no getting around the fact that a nonprofit organization *selling* shoes sounds a little strange. So many of us are used to charitable organizations only giving things away for free that there's an almost instinctive negative reaction to "sales." Yet, we have seen that this social enterprise model is not only financially sustainable for S4S; it is better for our entrepreneurial partners. They can count on us showing up month after month, not just when times are good. Because they are customers, not recipients, they have more dignity and equity in the relationship. They don't just have to take what we are offering but can push back for better pricing and product. I cannot overstate the confidence that comes from being treated as an equal.

But it's trickier than that. Because our corporate partners often require us to use their donations in specific locations, and we don't always have nonprofit partners in those places, we need for-profit distribution partners who play a key role collecting, processing, and shipping products, which allows us to be a good business partner to our brands and retailers. To their credit, those who first established the microenterprise model at S4S chose mostly great partners for the distribution piece, who are every bit as important as our direct 4Opportunity partners. The majority of them, people such as Kurt De Pourcq, Moe Haschem, Ali Haschem, and Steven Salstein, were not only quick to continue their support of our mission (remember that they helped finance S4S when we were nearly bankrupt); they have remained our partners a dozen years later and have generously offered philanthropic support to help fund new initiatives such as

4EveryKid. There is no way we could function without them. We are totally comfortable explaining this to our team, the board, and our donors. It's not as simple a story as "We give shoes to people in need"; the value is in the complexity, in how the people, partners, and products combine to create opportunity. Our indirect partners are for-profit, *and* they are aligned with our mission. Those things are not mutually exclusive, and, in a way, they require an even greater ability to articulate our "why," to be part of our entrepreneurial vision for how business can make a positive difference in the world, no matter your tax status.

Being entrepreneurial and being accountable run on parallel tracks. This requires us to have a vision that the team is greater than the individual; that collaboration is natural, useful, and rewarding; and that accountability to oneself and others changes us for the better. The entrepreneur's instinct to be a self-starter and a problem-solver began to permeate the organization. Not all the team members in place in 2012 had an interest in being held accountable or acting entrepreneurially. Those who didn't, chose to leave on their own accord as we began to change our organizational culture.

Of those who left, I think it is fair to say they were less mission-driven. By contrast, many of their colleagues had sought employment at S4S precisely because they believed in what we were trying to accomplish. That core value, "meaningful," is inextricably tied to mission, which is where we go next.

"STEPS" YOUR ORGANIZATION CAN TAKE

- Your organization has values, even if they're not written down. As a leader, one of your jobs is to make them visible and to be sure they are the ones you want to uphold.

- It is a leader's job to help shape values, not just name them. Listen and question, but have the courage to talk about what you think your organization's values should be and why. Once you've created some guardrails and issued a genuine invitation to participate in defining the values, you really can change the direction of the organization. It won't happen overnight, but it is worth the effort.

- An organization has to find multiple ways to reinforce its values. At S4S, we have someone share their take on a value at each of our Monday morning meetings. They are part of our quarterly and annual performance reviews. We sometimes let people go because they aren't aligned with our culture, even if their results are good.

- Never pass up an opportunity to use your values to talk about how to get better or celebrate someone's example. Values are something that we live by, not something we can wear out. In fact, it's the opposite ... the more you use them, the longer they last!

CHAPTER 5

Clarifying the Mission and Setting a Vision

> *Vision is a compass,
> not a road map.*
> **—PETER BLOCK**

How you frame your mission matters. It gives those outside of the organization a sense of who you are, and it serves as a compass for those on the inside. You can't fake it. If it's just a slogan, it's like a compass with no needle—it won't help you get where you want to go.

EVOLUTION AT WORK

Often, pictures are more powerful than words. This has been the case with the evolution of the S4S logo and tagline:

The first of these images was the logo and tagline S4S was using when I arrived. I cannot tell you how much I hate it. The halo most certainly did not align with an organization whose image had been severely tarnished. It also tried to play both sides of the field in terms of whether S4S was a faith-based organization. In trying to be cute, it came across as disingenuous, and it looked amateurish. There may have been initial value in the homespun aesthetic that S4S was a scrappy, relatable fighter and not a big corporate entity; but in 2012, we were at a hinge moment, and we needed to prove we were serious, open to everyone, and about more than handing out free shoes. This offered us a chance to rethink our mission. S4S had also become much more involved in apparel. "Changing the world one pair at a time" no longer captured the full range of the enterprise. As we contemplated our fuller vision, we had a little fun as we arrived at the tagline "Wearing out poverty," and we developed a cleaner, more professional logo. It was a visible sign that we were pulling out of the tailspin.

But within a few years, as we grew into a more capable, impactful organization, we asked ourselves whether that tagline still conveyed what we had become and still aspired to be. We reflected on what we had done best and what we could do next. Shoes and clothes supplied our entry point to "wearing out poverty," but wasn't the real point about how we helped turn those material items into *opportunities* that could change lives?

We asked ourselves and our supporters a series of questions to help us navigate to the next phase:

- How could we expand the transformation of basic products into more opportunities for entrepreneurs, providing them with a path to take care of themselves and their families, allowing them to grow, not just survive?
- How could we help further the missions of our nonprofit partners who worked so diligently to weave together a ragged social safety net by expanding access to education, nutrition, and housing, and especially creating economic opportunities for women?
- How could we create more opportunities for people to volunteer and to do something with their used shoes and clothes that made them feel better than leaving them in their closets or dumping them in landfills?
- What might be the long-term impact if we gave volunteers an opportunity to travel and experience our work directly?
- How could we increase engagement opportunities for the employees and customers of our corporate partners?
- How might we expand the opportunities of those partners to use their inventories for something more powerful than just selling for pennies on the dollar or, worst of all, destroying their product?
- How could we measure our impact in more comprehensive way so we understand what it means to those we serve?

Seeing our work through an impact lens allowed us to understand our role in the bigger story. Our tagline "Creating opportinity through shoes and clothing" is clear and speaks directly and holistically to our mission. The logo and tagline reflect an ethos that is down-to-earth, not flashy, which fits us. Shoes and clothes fulfill practical, everyday needs. The tagline and logo take a streamlined approach, which is something we strive for in our operations and communications. It's true that breaking the cycle of poverty is a huge, aspirational mission, something we are unlikely to ever achieve, no matter how successful we are. But to link such an aspirational goal with something as tangible as shoes and clothing provides a touchstone for us, something we can keep coming back to as we make our way in uncertain, changing times.

ANOTHER VOICE | **Nancy Youssef**

Nancy Youssef is a former board member of Soles4Souls and now serves as its chief business development officer and executive vice president, International. Prior to joining S4S, she was vice president, International Business Development for Genesco, Inc., where she pioneered the Fortune 1000 footwear and apparel retailer's portfolio of brands outside the United States.

Full Circle

I arrived on the Soles4Souls board early on, after Buddy became the CEO. From our first encounter, I recognized that we were connected by the mission. I was interested in the entrepreneurial piece of S4S, and the preponderance of my career had been in the footwear and apparel industry. We were also aligned in terms of values, particularly the international focus on combating poverty; in part, because I grew up all over the world, in a family of Egyptian background, and I had seen poverty and the need for shoes and clothing firsthand. I spent five years on the board, two as the chair; then when I stepped away and Buddy asked me to come to work on business development for S4S, I saw it as a chance to come full circle. When I arrived, I had two people on my team, and they were focused on corporate partnerships. Five years later I have twenty-five people on my team.

The full circle for me was that, by drawing on my background in business development and through working with the board, I saw the value of using the tools of shoes and clothing to create long-term wages. I realized that, for people to have the ability to be self-dependent and lift themselves out of poverty, they had to have the opportunity to learn skills that are transferable to other aspects of their lives. Working through our 4Opportunity program, we were participants in a process that literally impacts somebody's life for the long term; not just an immediate alteration but something that people can carry forward into other businesses and community support, and that they can pass on to the next generation. The knowledge entrepreneurs gain is sustainable. I have watched families who are engaged and kids who are engaged, and, one day soon, grandkids will be engaged, as entire communities are transformed and small economies are altered. It's never one and done. I've had the unusual opportunity to see this impact ten years on in places where we have forged partnerships.

I have traveled to most of the countries where we have 4Opporunity partners; yet, every time we meet with these entrepreneurs, every time I see the kids or the families who we're helping, it's life-altering. Every single time. It's never, "Oh, I've seen this movie before." And now, with 4EveryKid, we are witnessing similar transformations in our own backyard.

Unfortunately, disparity continues to grow, and need never goes away. We live in a country with so much abundance that sometimes people display a sense of entitlement or expectation, something that is brought home to me every time I travel overseas for S4S and see folks, from adults to children, in tattered clothing and with no shoes on their feet—or, if they have shoes, they are full of holes or their toes are hanging out because the shoes are too small. Being in a poor village is almost sensory overload. You see it, you feel it, you smell it. It can be overwhelming. But then there is a moment when you wash another person's feet and help them slip on a pair of new socks and place a pair of shoes on their feet, or find clothing that is their size, and the feeling is unbelievable. People are so humble, so cheerful. It is palpable. You can see the energy of excitement and happiness and genuine gratitude. They're ecstatic. Oftentimes, they immediately take the shoes off and say, "I'm saving these for Christmas." You don't have to speak the same language. You look in their eyes and understand their gratitude and see the difference something we take for granted has made in their lives.

CARRYING A COMPASS

A combination of big dreams and practical approaches can have value in any organization. It lets you make rapid decisions with clear guardrails. It keeps you on task. The concept of mission doesn't have to be front and center every moment of the workday when you're busy doing the work, but it provides a direction when we reach a fork in the trail. In 2013, when we acknowledged that a good portion of our warehouses were filled with a hodgepodge of inventory—wheelchairs, medical devices, and home goods—that had nothing to do with the markets we knew or the literal mission statement of "changing the world one pair at a time," the decision to get rid of all the clutter took no more than a nanosecond. We had the mission to guide us.

Focusing on our mission—creating opportunities for people using footwear and apparel—and linking to the impact we wanted S4S to achieve allowed us, just a few years later, to do what in 2012 would have seemed impossible: We took over another nonprofit that was in a tailspin. Founded in 2000 and based in Jacksonville, Florida, Dignity U Wear provided new, free shoes and clothing to tens of thousands of people each year through about one thousand charitable partner organizations. In 2017, one of our for-profit partners reached out to us. They had received a call from Dignity U Wear. The gist of the call to our partner was, "Hey, we're in real trouble. We've been selling stuff that we shouldn't have been selling. We had permission to donate it for free, but we desperately needed the money, so we sold it." An executive from one of Dignity U Wear's big donors was on vacation in the Caribbean and saw items they had donated for sale. In an eerily familiar scenario, right down to the larger financial problems that led to Dignity U Wear making such a decision, the situation created an existential crisis. Our indirect partner told them, "You should talk to Soles4Souls. They were in trouble like this a few years ago. They might be able to help guide you."

With Bernadette's help, David, Robert Adams-Ghee (who had joined us that year as our CFO), and I quickly dug into learning as much as we could about Dignity U Wear. As we spoke with several members of its board, it became immediately clear that they recognized that Dignity U Wear had reached its end, and they were looking to merge with an entity that could continue its original mission and service several of the organizations with which it had developed long relationships. We saw the obvious mission alignment and, moreover, recognized that, with an acquisition, we could expand our presence in the apparel ecosystem.

Our due diligence was sound. The people at Dignity U Wear were serious and upstanding. We saw that the opportunities outweighed any deficits, and we were able to move quickly. Dignity U Wear also saw the mission alignment, and in the merger, they gave us their entire inventory and a building they had intended to sell but that was suffering from serious environmental liabilities. We brought two of their board members onto our board and made good on our commitments to honor relationships with the key organizations they identified. Nearly eight years later, we continue to serve those organizations. We also sold the building. Ultimately, we were able to carry out a healthy, productive combination because we had clarity around what we were doing, and why—something that would not have been possible without a clear sense of where we were headed.

ANOTHER VOICE | **Parker McCrary**

Parker McCrary is an emeritus board member of Soles4Souls and the former board chair of the Dignity U Wear Foundation. A career C-suite professional in the transportation industry, he is currently the deputy program manager for HTNB Freight and Logistics Planning.

A Happy Merger

Dignity U Wear was founded by Henri Landwirth, a Holocaust survivor, hotelier, and serial philanthropist. Henri was an extraordinary guy, and everyone who knew him wanted a little bit of his time. All *he* wanted was to help people, to go hang out at the homeless shelter, talk to those folks, and ask them, "What do you really need? What can I do to change your life?" Their answer was, "We need socks. We need underwear." From those simple roots, Dignity U Wear grew into an organization that supplied donated clothing to people in multiple states, distributed through nonprofits with which we had deep relationships. We created a network of people from Cantor Fitzgerald and elsewhere on Wall Street, who started fundraising for us. We received donations from brands such as Izod, Van Heusen, Brooks Brothers, and Coach, and we sought advice from fashion industry experts through an advisory board we formed. Our core mission was to help other nonprofits do what they did, but better. We became quite successful because of the wealth of networks we established. But what Dignity U Wear didn't have was an economic model that would allow us to keep the lights on. We could get all the nicest clothes, handbags, purses ... you name it ... but it cost money to get them to people. A lot of money. It's hard for a nonprofit to just have its hands out all the time and expect somebody else to keep the lights on. This can work for a little while, but it's hard to be sustainable this way.

By 2017, we saw we had reached the limits of what we could sustain, and that was when we encountered interest from Soles4Souls. They had figured out the revenue part of how to turn donated goods into economic opportunity. We saw the intelligence in their model and the alignment of our two missions. A lot of their work had been focused internationally, and we saw an opportunity in the merger to increase the national impact of our shared missions. I told Buddy when we agreed to the merger, "I come with the package. I want to be on the Soles4Souls board. I'm going to hold you accountable to your commitments." Soles-4Souls' response was great. They retained the New York advisory committee, which they maintain to this day. The committee is worth its weight in gold because it is formed of apparel industry experts who work right in the heart of the NYC Garment District.

Dignity U Wear had benefited greatly from the advisory committee, and we had also learned a lot about the logistics involved in fulfilling our mission, particularly when it came to crisis relief and understanding where clothing donations stand in the priority list after a natural disaster. That knowledge was one of several things Dignity U Wear brought to Soles4Souls. My term

> serving on the board was both instructive and rewarding. We were necessarily a "working board" in those days, and I developed a tremendous fondness and respect for the S4S team and my fellow board members. It was one of those unique circumstances in which I felt I received as much as I gave. This was true in large part because, just as I had at Dignity U Wear, I totally believed—*believe*; I still do and I still feel very connected—in their mission.

No journey, of a business, an organization, a movement, or an individual, occurs in a straight line. Rivers flood. Bridges get knocked out. Restructuring eliminates positions. Things break down. People die. Because you will be forced to find your way around the unexpected, because some of your waypoints will change over time, you need two critical items: a destination, however aspirational, and a good compass to give you a heading. You still need grit and perseverance, but wherever you may find yourself on your journey, having a clear mission increases your odds of getting where you want to go.

As for the compass, it's a very important tool. But it only points the way. You have to find a "how." It could be walking, a horse, or a 4x4, but you need to move from dream to reality. For us, it was all about a robust operating system. That's where we go next.

"STEPS" YOUR ORGANIZATION CAN TAKE

- Your mission is a compass, not a map. It's critical in making decisions but not usually a day-to-day tool.

- Visions don't change very often; your mission might. Be open to the idea that how you talk about your mission will evolve, and adapt when you need to.

- Mission is a team sport. Creating one should reflect input from important stakeholders and be relatable to your entire organization.

- Missions should both close doors (what you won't do) and open them (what's possible and acceptable to do). If your mission doesn't help you say "no" to some things, you probably don't have it nailed down yet.

- Vision is critical, but it won't get you there. It's like getting in a car with a clear destination but no map or fuel. Without those, you're not going to make much progress. The real power of the mission is when you put it into action.

CHAPTER 6

Implementing a Robust Operating System

You do not rise to the level of your goals.
You fall to the level of your systems.
—JAMES CLEAR, ATOMIC HABITS

A few years ago, I happened upon the budget for fiscal year 2011—a budget cycle two years before my arrival. It was one page, no details. Because my predecessor had secured such a large grant early on, I think it was easy for the executive team to grow complacent about finances and budgeting in the belief they had plenty of money. As I have detailed, things were far from fine. The connection between their bare-bones budgeting processes and the financial reality was hard to ignore.

When it became clear how bad things were with S4S's systems, finances, and people, I knew we had to find and implement a different way to organize our thinking immediately. I've known Verne Harnish since the early nineties, and in 2002, he published a terrific book, *Mastering the Rockefeller Habits*, based on Rockefeller's weekly luncheon meetings with his top lieutenants. Verne built on Rockefeller's meeting rhythms, and from this, he created a framework for how to organize and stay on top of your business. (In 2014, he wrote another excellent book, *Scaling Up*, that expanded on these principles.) I recognized that we needed a way to make better, faster decisions if S4S was going to survive. David, Les, and I would lead the turnaround, and this would be our road map. Les Ward, with whom I had worked when he was CFO at the YPO, was also cofounder of a turnaround consulting firm, which made him a great fit. We challenged ourselves to start the reorganization by asking, "Why are we doing this? What are our targets?" A big part of *Scaling Up* is the one-page strategic plan. On one sheet of legal paper, you establish your purpose, values, north star, three-to-five-year capabilities, and one-year initiatives, right down to what you'll do this quarter. Essentially, the goal is to create a snapshot that says, "This is who we are, where we're going, and how we're going to get there."

The first year, I filled out the page mostly by myself. Then, I discovered that a network had grown up around *Mastering the Rockefeller Habits* that had created a support system of certified coaches. Those who had developed this support system recognized that it is impossible for a CEO or even an active leadership team to scale a company all on their own. I found a certified coach in North Carolina. Because we had no money to travel to him or to bring him to us, we conducted our conversations by phone, something that was far from ideal but still allowed us to have conversations focused on the framework and gave me something more than simply implementing my own applications of the book. A year later, as we made incremental progress in our finances and our operations, we reached a point at which we were able to secure the expertise of the Nashville consulting company Petra Coach. For several years, we worked with a coach named Gene Robertson, who helped us successfully navigate hard times and significant growth. Since 2022, Bill Hankins has been instrumental in our continued development. There is a huge advantage in having a coach who knows the organization well but is not an insider. A coach can ask the hard questions without having a personal stake that's tied to the incentives a team member who wants to preserve a bonus or earn a promotion might have. They can be objective and use that objectivity to push an organization harder.

Now, rather than feeling isolated in developing strategic goals, our whole leadership team (and, yes, along with other organizational improvements, we have an excellent, highly professional leadership team today) comes together once a quarter to undertake a structured process of answering the questions in the one-page strategic plan. In our quarterly sessions, we determine our top three organizational priorities. We tackle big, strategic stuff, and then we come right down to what's going to happen in the next ninety days, who will be accountable for each objective, and what agreed metric we'll use to evaluate our success. This rhythm creates discipline, transparency, and accountability around what we're doing and what needs attention. It's a recipe for constant improvement.

Before establishing a framework, S4S had a culture in which one answer to a strategic plan question might apply to one team while another would receive a completely different answer. By starting at our BHAG for 2030, then three-year initiatives, then a one-year plan, we're able to set, track, and evaluate quarterly and annual progress. This waterfall of timelines and targets ensures we have one eye on the long term and one on the here and now, allowing us to be tactical and strategic, practical and ambitious in the right time frames. It's a constant reference for us so that we have the bigger picture of where we're headed to inform all of those smaller decisions along the way.

ANOTHER VOICE | Bill Hankins

Bill Hankins is a certified business coach with Petra, a global coaching organization that empowers leaders and their teams to scale. After serving as a Special Assistant United States Attorney, he earned an MBA, held executive leadership roles in growth-stage organizations, and now helps entrepreneurs and CEOs to navigate the intricate landscape of business growth and organizational scaling.

In Alignment

Coaching plays a pivotal role in guiding CEOs and leadership teams to establish and maintain strategic alignment, enhance communication, promote accountability, and boost productivity across organizations. With Soles4Souls, I and my Petra colleagues have coached the leadership team in a time of exciting growth. We have worked together to help them build a culture that not only drives performance but also enables scalability. Bringing an outside, third-party perspective is an asset in the coaching relationship. It allows us to assess challenges and opportunities with a fresh and unbiased perspective—avoiding a "We've always done it like this" mentality. Another benefit is the cross-pollination of ideas that comes with coaching exposure to other organizations in different industries—sharing innovative practices that might not have otherwise been considered. Petra has an unwavering commitment to seeing that S4S taps into unrealized potential within the organization so that they can create opportunity for people.

One of the first steps in building a strong performance culture in any organization is ensuring the team is aligned around a clear strategy. Petra aids this alignment by guiding leadership teams through the process of creating a clear and concise one-page strategic plan, which serves as a simple yet powerful tool to guide the entire organization. Coaches also work with teams to implement structured daily, weekly, and monthly communication rhythms, ensuring that important information flows efficiently and accurately. Establishing the right communication rhythms is key, as it allows team members to stay informed and aligned with the company's goals.

Accountability is crucial for ensuring that each team member takes ownership of their roles and outcomes. This sense of ownership is not just about individual performance; it's also about creating a culture in which high standards are maintained and reliability becomes a hallmark. By promoting accountability, the team works together toward common goals, driving continuous improvement. Defining clear key performance indicators (KPI) allows the team to measure progress and ensure efforts are directed toward achieving the organization's broader objectives. By fostering a commitment to continuous improvement, the team can constantly refine their strategies and workflows, ensuring sustained growth.

A key tool that supports this approach is the use of an accountability management platform such as Align. Such platforms are extremely useful for both strategic alignment and monitoring progress toward individual and company priorities that support the strategic plan. Align helps separate the "in the business" work from the "on the business" work. When these platforms become part of a team's operational infrastructure, they serve to keep everyone focused on the key goals for the quarter, year, and beyond. When you have a progress-tracking feature to hold team members accountable to accomplish the goals they committed to, it elevates productivity. Everyone wants to end the quarter in the green!

Soles4Souls has done a superb job implementing the functionality of Align and adopting processes and systems to drive communication, strategic alignment, and accountability. Organizations such as S4S that employ an operating system based on these principles can achieve remarkable progress. S4S uses quarterly planning sessions to assess its performance, revisit its core values, and set clear priorities for the upcoming period. These sessions are not just a formality; they are a vital part of ensuring everyone is working toward a unified objective. The process has helped S4S stay focused on its strategic goals, course-correct when necessary, and create a foundation for sustainable growth.

Ultimately, the combination of a strong performance culture, clear strategic alignment, and a robust operating system has created an environment in which S4S has thrived.

OPENING THE CHANNELS FOR COLLABORATION

Our executive team huddles briefly in a ten- to twenty-minute meeting four days a week. We start by asking if there is anyone we should recognize from the previous day, then we cover key items from the day before and briefly outline our focus for the day, including our top priorities. When we first proposed such regular huddles, some of our executive team members thought we were crazy. After doing it for years now, team members who can remember what it was like before we held such regular check-ins ask, "How did we work without a daily huddle?" I know that without these daily, weekly, quarterly, and annual rhythms, we would never have been able to conceive, launch, and scale a new program like 4EveryKid. Without a strategy and planning framework in place, we tend to focus on the "right now." A framework not only sparks such conversations; it also creates a culture in which we know we are in something together and we have to push one another to achieve objectives we've all had a hand in establishing. With this structure in place, we discovered a rhythm that completely changed our culture. We now have the means to discuss, consistently and with purpose, who we are serving and how we can serve them better.

 ANOTHER VOICE | **Randy Dunn**

Randy Dunn spent thirty-eight years with UPS in organizational leadership, strategy, operations, regulatory compliance, and state and government affairs while leading, managing, and motivating diverse teams of more than fifteen thousand people. He is the chief strategy officer for DBH Distributing and an emeritus board member of Soles4Souls.

I joined the Soles4Souls board when there was truly little more than pixie dust keeping the organization together. We were a group of hard-hitting, hard-charging businesspeople who always tell it like it is. We became extremely close-knit and functioned almost like unpaid employees as we helped Buddy restructure. We took on this oversized role because we believed in the intent, the purpose, and the strategies. That cohesive group of board members was instrumental in supporting Buddy with the strategy ahead. It was magic. Every month, every quarter, we saw gains. With time, the board was able to step back and advise and focus on governance, as nonprofit boards are intended.

As a six-year board member and the chair of the finance committee administering Buddy's pay, I always felt that it was my role to be overtly candid with Buddy. It was (and has remained) a wide-open relationship of candor, frankness, and tough love. I'm a "lead-from-behind" guy who doesn't like the spotlight but understands systems and knows how to interact with people individually.

In one-on-one settings, I was very forthcoming with Buddy about things that needed to change, the strategies required to create more accountability and structure, and the importance of putting operational systems in place that we needed in order to deliver on our mission.

With Buddy's leadership, alongside that of people such as David Graben and Robert Adams-Ghee, combined with a talented board that understood strategy, S4S turned around quickly considering how bad the problems had gotten (although it didn't seem quick at the time). When I joined, our auditors were about to fire S4S. The company's inventory systems were so inadequate that they didn't want to put their name on the line. While the organization knew it had to move past spreadsheets, there was no money to fund the right kind of technology. Still, the board pushed to get a rudimentary system in place. Along with upgrading from QuickBooks, we kept the auditors on board. Those kinds of actions were furthered with the hiring of Robert as CFO, and as the board treasurer and finance committee chair, we were able to work in concert and talked almost weekly about the financial prudence of the organization and where we needed to go.

The transformation of S4S is a storyline of polar opposites. In a matter of a less than a decade, the organization went from being at risk of not making payroll and unable to purchase the software and logistics infrastructure it needed to properly run, to being able to create an investment fund that it one day might be able to convert into an endowment. It's just a huge, huge success story.

Acting on our belief in transparency, we make all of our company priorities visible to everyone in the organization right in our daily dashboard. We take it a step further and create a hierarchy in those priorities so that everyone knows what our number one target is. We have extended this idea deeper into our culture by asking every team member to identify their number one individual priority. If this approach has been good for the organization, why wouldn't it be good for the individuals within it? Just as some company priorities can be tied to hard targets such as revenue growth, so can some individual targets. More often, the priority and success metric are unique to the role the individual holds, but the *process* of establishing priorities and a means to measure their achievement creates change that we can build on.

Before every quarterly planning meeting—and I cannot stress how important this day-long session is—all leadership team members complete a survey that asks them to identify

1. colleagues they believe should be recognized,
2. what worked last quarter,
3. what didn't work,
4. the feeling of the team,
5. the top three organizational priorities they think we should focus on, and
6. their top three quarterly individual priorities.

Then, as a leadership team, we work through this together so that we can find where we're aligned and what points we need to discuss further. I firmly believe that such a process has allowed us to move the organization forward while also allowing everyone to see all they have accomplished quarter to quarter, year over year. When our team sees sustained personal and professional growth, not only do they feel accomplished and part of something bigger; they also get excited for future opportunities.

In 2012, only a few people knew much about what was really happening financially, programmatically, or managerially. This is not true at S4S today. We post our financials every morning. There's a KPI dashboard that tells us exactly where we are on donations; how many footwear units we have on hand; how many apparel units are in our warehouse; and how those measurements align with our quarterly, annual, and three-year targets. There's no place to hide. My personal priorities are visible to the whole organization, as are those of our team member who answers the phones. And everyone can see if I've checked my priorities as complete. This level of accountability and transparency courses throughout the organization. By having everyone's priorities and progress public, we have a way to talk about where we stand both as an organization and as individuals. We are able to use the transparency Align allows us to discuss whether an objective was accomplished or not, what we learned along the way, and what we will do differently next time.

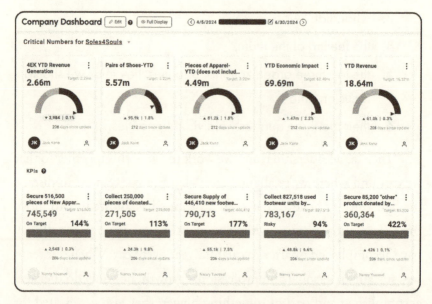

Screenshot of the company dashboard in Align.

ANOTHER VOICE | **Mike Shirey**

Mike Shirey joined the Soles4Souls team as chief operating officer in 2020, bringing over twenty-five years of retail and wholesale experience in the footwear industry. Prior to joining S4S, Mike held various senior executive roles leading premium wholesale, design, and planning and sourcing teams at Aerosoles, Nine West, Highline United, and Nina Shoes.

Fan-Damn-Tastic!

It's important to know that the COO role at Soles4Souls isn't a typical one. Here, there is one KPI you might expect—earned revenue (the *real* dollars we must generate to pay the team and function). But we have another KPI—economic impact (a measurement of how effective S4S is at being on mission). This metric, while a very real economic measurement of how well we have used our donations to help people escape the cycle of poverty, is *not real* dollars. After nearly twenty-six years in the retail and wholesale women's footwear market, my career experience had largely prepared me for the commercialization of the inventory aspect of the job through years of sales and operations management, but the economic impact metric and how best to create robust, people-empowering programming was a whole new world. Once I figured that out, I was able to bring out my genuine love of helping people and building teams and balance that with the commercial toughness that's required to make sure S4S isn't being taken advantage of.

When I arrived, S4S didn't have an integrated system. It had five different platforms that didn't connect to one another, and it was way more difficult to run the company the way it needed to be. In late 2022, we started the process of reviewing potential enterprise resource planning (ERP) systems. I led the ERP project team along with our CFO, and it was an incredibly entrepreneurial process from start to rollout in May 2024. Our core values were on full display throughout the ERP rollout. Converting a fragmented and archaic system to integrated software and a modern operating system required plenty of practice in transparency and entrepreneurship. I remember one session with our Netsuite rollout team and our Accounting Manager David Briggs—who is famously loud and direct (in the best way)—when he realized that we were going to be able to generate invoices directly from the system without an email being received (which was created from a handwritten note from the warehouse floor), and he employed one of our CFO's favorite phrases: "That's Fan-Damn-Tastic!" Everyone on the rollout team shared a similar excited, if nervous, spirit and pulled together.

A new ERP system was one important tool in building a larger, more effective operating system. What I had been doing for the last twenty-plus years was very useful as we started to plan the product flow and impact measurement by month and quarter. I created waves when I insisted on a big change in philosophy. S4S had long been operating on a "survive day to day" mentality, which resulted in rushing donations out the door in order to speed up receipt of payment (the needed earned revenue KPI). I thought we had a lot to gain by adopting a more "intentionally review the donation and place it with the right partner" philosophy. This change in philosophy was *painful* for everyone at first, no doubt. We had to centralize the decision-making and then ensure we really were making the best match of donation to partner. This change allowed S4S to benefit more on revenue generation as we started to get better value for the 4Opportunity donations *and* the right partners in need were receiving the right product!

An operating system that fits your organization perfectly will still be useless without a quality team that knows how to use it to the greatest advantage. That's where we go next.

"STEPS" YOUR ORGANIZATION CAN TAKE

- There is not one right operating system. What can seem magical is finding one that fits your organization. A major part of a "proper fit" is finding an approach that aligns with your values as well as your needs.

- Talk with leaders at other organizations that either have similar needs or similar values, or that are of a similar size. Find peers with whom you can have regular conversations about how your organizations operate.

- No one works well in a vacuum. And meetings don't have to last for hours. Find rhythms that work for your organization. Whether your teams work remotely, in-person, or on a hybrid basis, team members needed mechanisms that allow them to work collaboratively and that create frequent opportunities for regular check-ins with each other and their managers.

- Good operating systems have accountability built in. With everyone on the same system, used appropriately, you can get everyone on the same page.

CHAPTER 7

Building a Strong Team

*A player who makes a team great
is better than a great player.*
—JOHN WOODEN

In 2012, there were people on the S4S team who thought that my predecessor was a visionary. Others felt betrayed by him. Most were simply trying to figure out what was going on. Once I was announced as the new CEO, and with the gradual awakening among team members of just how deep the S4S financial hole had become, everyone in the organization felt uncertain about whether they would still have a job. While many were deeply devoted to the S4S mission, belief in the value of your work alone doesn't feed your kids or pay the mortgage. Their concern was understandable and justified.

There were several additional factors that added to the uncertainty. As I have shared, David Graben was the interim CEO when I arrived, and he wanted the job permanently, so our start together wasn't exactly "Hey, let's be pals and run this thing together." (As our partnership and friendship developed, he changed his mind. Eventually, he said, "Being CEO sucks. I love being the COO!") The previous year or so, as the chaos had begun ramping up, so had the rumor mill. It was hard to get a read on the mood, but I'd say there were a lot of folks occupying the narrow space between "He won't last" and "It won't work."

The truth is that I didn't help my own transition. I had (mostly) lived in Dallas since 1988. We had two young daughters in school. Starting after the school year had begun wasn't feasible, so the plan was to move the following summer. The board was totally supportive, and I started commuting most weeks, along with lots of travel to visit partners, donors, and industry events. While the team understood the short-term commuting plan, I had a personal crisis that ended up sending a very different message. My wife, Becca, and I had been partners in marriage and parenting for twenty years. But we misread each other about the move to Nashville. After I started to realize how precarious the organization's financial situation was, Becca was adamant about not moving until our youngest daughter finished the eighth grade ... which wouldn't be until 2016! There is no question that this was one of the low points of our marriage. Many of you will know the stress travel puts on the traveler and their family. For me, this was turbocharged because, just a few months in, I was going to break a promise to the board about my timing to relocate. Definitely grist for the rumor mill.

With my stomach churning, I let the board know in March 2013 that I couldn't move my family to Nashville for a few years. Braced for the worst, but knowing I had to model transparency in such a crucial moment, I shared that information, expecting a brutal conversation about my future. Instead, I heard a huge, collective exhale! The board fully understood that the chaos at S4S was real and that survival was still a coin toss. They were relieved that I wasn't going to uproot my family, and they had been weighing how they might say that to me without seeming too negative. It's funny now, but it sure wasn't then.

But for many on the team, it seemed as though I was hedging my bets, not making a commitment. Even though I knew I was in it for the long haul, that's not how it looked from the outside. I got that eventually, but I was blind to it at the time. And it mattered. One of the executive team members used it to take shots at me behind my back, undermining confidence in me and what we were trying to do. It took a few months for me to believe that was happening, but when it did, I let him go. There was a performance component, for sure, but the biggest reason was misalignment with our still-being-articulated values. It was not my primary reason, but I wasn't unaware of the message it sent: The old way of doing business at S4S was over. We were reinvigorating the team and the organization, and I was here to be a part of that for years to come.

One of the first footwear industry trips was to New York City, about a month after I started. It would prove to be one of my lowest points at S4S. Every person I met was a stranger to me, yet they all knew the public circumstances that had brought me to my new job. My head was spinning. I wondered, *What am I doing here?* I was walking down the street—and this was right after Hurricane Sandy, so there was another layer of chaos going on around me in the literal sense—when my phone rang. It was our controller, Tim Deats. "Buddy," he said, "the bank pulled our line of credit and seized our collateral. We have no money."

I thought, *Well, hell. I knew we were broke, but at least we had access to credit.* We could fix a lot of things, but this didn't feel like one of them. And I was about to enter an event filled with footwear executives we would be dependent on if we had any chance. I thought, *This thing might already be over.* I was left simultaneously wondering how I could ensure people who had supported S4S that we were confident we could turn it around and how I would tell my wife that this new journey—one she wasn't yet fully on board with—might be over before it started.

CREATING THE CULTURE WE WANT

On my arrival, we had sixty-two employees. Over the next two years, through attrition and asking some people to leave, we shrank to thirty-seven. Those who stayed on learned how to be lean and to step up in unfamiliar roles when a teammate needed help. The only incentive we could offer was togetherness; the feeling that came with everyone pitching in to save something we knew could do good. For a number of years, because there simply was no money, we did away with bonuses. When we reached a level of financial stability that allowed us to bring them back, bonuses were based on the organization's performance rather than individual performance. This was a big change because bonuses had previously been paid even when S4S was hemorrhaging cash! We would fail or succeed as a team. At S4S, our view is that if someone is not pulling their weight, it's a manager's job to figure that out rather than primarily relying on an incentive structure to generate engagement. We focused on creating an environment that supported people who wanted to work there.

Today, we have more than eighty exceptionally qualified team members who manage an organization that dwarfs what it once was in terms of revenue, people served, and economic impact. We're

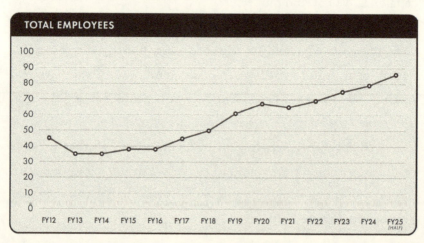

extremely proud that we pay bonuses, offer fair salaries, and provide quality benefits that include a 6% 401(k) match and cover 75% of health insurance premiums. We think about the things we can do that can take stress off our employees. We hope to do more, but we're committed to treating people fairly.

It seems obvious to me that we need to make a commitment to our team if we want them to make a commitment to Soles4Souls. We ask our people for a lot of work and pay them fairly, but we recognize we cannot match what they might earn at a for-profit enterprise. One of our values is "meaningful," and that includes ensuring the work each team member does is meaningful to them and those we serve. While you can't feed your family on values, knowing your work makes a difference is not nothing. Purpose is one of the ways we make sense out of our work, and we're intentional about making this explicit.

A great example of this was when the pandemic hit. We're all familiar with the atmosphere in 2020 as people throughout the country were losing their jobs. At S4S, we told our team that we were not laying anyone off because of COVID-19. Thanks to lessons learned from our tailspin, we had built an operating reserve to get through an unforeseen crisis. We were able to assure our team that no one would be losing their job for at least a year. There were enough other things to be scared about without people fearing for their jobs, so we took that off the table. I'm really proud of that. To me, this showed commitment going both ways—we didn't just say, "Give more; work harder." We practiced putting on our own oxygen masks first. I'm happy to say that, with the exception of David dying, not one person left S4S from March 2020 through August 2021.

But talking about values and fairness was not enough. We needed systems that reinforced them. For example, we learned that annual reviews didn't work for us. They created a high-stakes, high-stress, artificial moment. Who can remember what happened twelve months ago to effectively evaluate someone's performance? Nancy Youssef, our chief business development officer, simply started doing quarterly performance reviews and made them much more conversational. She saw great results, so we implemented them for the entire organization. If we want our team members to grow, it makes more sense to create opportunities to talk more often and less formally; to have conversations rather than litmus tests. We set identifiable and transparent targets for performance evaluation. In some parts of the organization, these can be straightforward and quantitative. For example, our business development team knows where we want to be in three years, in one year, and each quarter. They have corresponding targets for the number of used shoes, used apparel, new shoes, new apparel, etc. that they need to bring in for each of those periods. Our fundraising and operations teams have similar, unambiguous targets. In parts of the business where being quantitative doesn't work, we set clear, realistic benchmarks that keep folks accountable. For example, rather than HR simply stating they will fill a vacant position, we ask that they define, and meet, specific target actions, such as hire date, start date, and completion date for onboarding. All of this ties back to our quarterly planning meetings, when we set measurable goals so that we can really know if each of us is honoring the commitment we have made to ourselves and the organization.

BUILDING A STRONG TEAM

ANOTHER VOICE | **Kelly Modena**

Kelly Modena started working for Soles4Souls as a fundraiser in 2011 and then oversaw its community partnerships programs for several years, with a particular emphasis on the 4Opportunity program. She is currently the chief of staff for S4S.

Unity in Purpose

I've worn a lot of hats for Soles4Souls, starting as a fundraiser, growing a faith-based donation campaign, developing our community partnership programs and organizing shoe drives ... you name it and I've probably done it. Throughout my time at S4S, I've been driven by my passion. I've shown up at bat mitzvahs and bar mitzvahs and mud runs and school gyms to collect shoes. My passion motivated me even in 2012 when a lot of team members were jumping ship. When Buddy arrived, our team was so thin and so shaken that we were all wearing about eight thousand hats, but his no-nonsense approach to gossip, and his asking us, "Who are we really? What's our core purpose?" shifted our mindset. In answering those questions, almost immediately, it felt like there weren't so many hats. Buddy set the model from the start because we saw how he had taken such a huge risk in choosing to lead a dying organization in a new city far from his family. And yet, he checked his pride at the door, got down to work, and inspired us to believe S4S was worth saving. We realized that we had a *lot* to do, but not only did we really want to see S4S survive—we also felt united as a team.

This sense of unity is a result of the larger culture we have established. You can't have unity without being vulnerable and transparent; something that is in just about everything we do. Every

Monday, at our staff meeting, someone is responsible for talking about one of our core values. It gives us the chance to share a story about a team member or a partner that was inspirational or something we faced when our values saved us. It can be powerful, but it's still nerve-racking, simply because you have to be vulnerable in public. But talking about our core values together is one of those opportunities to make sure we live by them. It gives us a voice in our culture. This is something S4S does well—providing a platform to be heard and then listening to what we say. Team members regularly complete surveys, which gives them the opportunity to rate our organization, so leadership can keep a pulse on our team. The results are discussed by our leadership team, and if they see that a problem exists, they look for solutions. It's a culture in which your whole team wants you to succeed. They also want you to be happy. Our mission is all about helping people, and our leadership team and our board are great about wanting to help us so that we can help others.

Values at S4S aren't just words posted on a flyer in a breakroom. We live by them. Our core values have completely transformed our team. I had two babies *before* we had a maternity leave plan. And honestly, realizing that I had no time off to be with my children after their births made me feel like a victim of my desire to have a family because I was left on my own to figure out how to find care for my kids. A whole generation of employees was left scrambling. I had to apply for short-term disability. Others needed to turn to family members for help. But once S4S began to transform financially and we developed an organizational culture in which we could talk about our need to balance our lives with our work, we encountered an executive team that was open to discussing the issue. At the time, that team was made up mostly of men, and to their credit, not only did they hear our needs; they made a commitment to change. They developed a maternity leave policy and, soon after, included paternity leave. They showed that they were accountable to their team.

Accountability has a huge trickle-down effect. Seeing it at a leadership level, it creates a spirit that has only fueled my passion more, and I appreciate the autonomy I am provided to be entrepreneurial. Our teams are effective in large part because they are provided with clear goals but are given the freedom to create their own solutions to reach them and the comfort of knowing there will always be others to help.

I'm lucky. I get to spend my days around great people, working toward a powerful cause. And guess what? We have a lot of fun doing it.

TRUSTING OUR CULTURE
IN A BRAVE NEW WORLD

When the world abruptly transformed in 2020 and the pandemic forced us to work remotely, we didn't have to invent something to create connectivity when we went virtual. Because of our operating systems, we already knew what people were working on and what they were prioritizing. Our ability to support remote work effectively allowed us to expand and make new remote hires, including a major international expansion. We now have team members in more than twenty US states and six countries. Suddenly, rather than trying to find the best person from Nashville, we could hire the best talent from anywhere. We had to figure out how to make up for the gap of not having frequent in-person contact, which has made things such as our annual retreats even more critical. There, we work intentionally to get people plugged in and energized. It's imperfect, but it can be offset by team members who are highly productive in remote roles, appreciative of the flexibility remote working brings them, and happier in other aspects of their lives, which makes them more centered. Since we went totally remote in December 2020 (with the exception of our warehouses), we have had three of our four best years ever. Being remote has also helped us drive other goals, such as completely revamping our onboarding process, which I don't think we would have done had we still been in-person only. There are trade-offs, but there's no going back for us.

In fact, the approach we took to improve onboarding is illustrative of how we have shifted our vision of what makes an effective team. We first thought about onboarding from the perspective of the essential, mechanical/logistical stuff: "How do I get paid? Where's my computer? What are my software credentials?" All of this is covered two weeks prior to the start date. Every task is mapped out with the team member responsible for each item. Then we move on to the "how."

- How do we get shoes to Alabama?
- How do shoes and clothes get from California to Moldova?
- What's a direct partner?
- What's economic impact?
- Why do we only provide new shoes and clothes for free?
- And. So. Much. More.

There's a lot to cover, and only after new team members have some context are they prepared to have meaningful conversations about *why* we do what we do. Coming out of a quarterly priority, we now have a thirty-/sixty-/ninety-day onboarding plan that spells it all out. This is how we keep reinforcing the value of setting priorities;

everyone sees priorities come to life, which makes a difference for new members of the team.

Organizations are more complicated than they used to be. Even though S4S is small in the grand scheme, we're a global organization. But the more spread out you are, the more you've got to get the culture right to avoid people feeling isolated. Team members want to feel valued. They want to be seen as individuals. Little things matter because getting them wrong is like putting sand in the gears—it's hard to see, but it wears everyone down.

Here's a simple example. Recently, two of our US-based team members were coordinating with a colleague in the Netherlands. As part of their planning for our annual retreat, themed "Going Global" (the irony is not lost on me), one of the US colleagues proposed that we create a bingo game in order to make an activity more interactive. The team member from the Netherlands said, "I think I know the game you're talking about, but I'm not sure." It's a tiny thing, but her point was an important one that we all encounter in our workplaces with regularity: the assumptions we make about what people know and how they perceive communications. The three talked about the importance of an open atmosphere that allowed them to learn and consider cultural nuances. It's a huge thing in our business, not just because we have team members all over the world but because, as I have discussed, the approaches we take in acting on our mission in one country are not the same as they are in another. This point was driven home even further when they decided they could provide the winner of their game with a prize. One of the US colleagues suggested they could offer gift cards. The Netherlands team member said, "Well, that's thoughtful, but gift cards don't work here." She meant that literally; countries in the EU cannot honor gift cards issued in the US, even if some of the same retailers operate in both places. The intention was pure. It might be little more than a ten-dollar gift card provided in the fun of a game during training, but the subtle message the employee takes away could be, "You didn't think about where I live or how this might get used." This is a perception that can turn corrosive, despite good intentions.

You can't know how someone is feeling unless you create a place where they feel they can talk and be heard. Because we are a small organization, I have the ability to know everyone who works for us. When we make a new hire, after they've had a few weeks to settle, I talk to them. I keep it informal and conversational, and we get to know each other a bit so we become two people rather than extensions of our titles. But the main thing I ask is this: "We managed to sell you on Soles4Souls. Now that you've been here a few weeks, what's different from what we sold you?" They get to see that we are serious about transparency, and we get a fresh set of eyes on the organization.

REMEMBERING WHY WE EXIST

If Tim Deats's call to me while I was walking down a NYC sidewalk was a memorable low point, a formative high point came only weeks later. In January 2013, I traveled to Haiti for the first time, along with my wife and two daughters. I'd been consumed by the problems at S4S and suddenly found myself in a country where the worst of our problems was a daydream compared to the harsh daily reality of the Haitian people. The official unemployment rate in Haiti is high, and there aren't many jobs in the formal sector, so everyone has to be an entrepreneur, which counts as unemployed. You have to hustle just to stay alive.

We'd had a long day of travel and giving away shoes, and we were driving back to our hotel in the dark. And I mean *dark*. There weren't any streetlights, just the occasional generator powering dim bulbs in little stores and fires burning in barrels. Yet, everywhere, people were still out selling. I turned to Kesnel "Paul" Toussaint, our Haitian trip leader, and asked, "Why are they still out here in the dark?"

"They haven't earned enough to eat for today."

I had arrived with an unarticulated, partially formed belief that Haitian people were lazy. I'm ashamed to write those words now. What I found were people who worked a thousand times harder than I had at any point in my life. Haitians will do whatever it takes to care for their children. In a flash, it occurred to me that I was surrounded by people who didn't need to be taught how to work; they needed better products to sell. We had just begun talking with Sam Darguin, but in that moment, I could see the path forward.

I understood how the rudimentary model that had been at the root of the S4S controversy, if smartly managed and allowed to evolve, could become the lift people needed to improve their lives. I also got a humbling lesson in how much I needed to learn—about poverty, about the will of people to raise themselves up, about the nuances of philanthropy, the complexities of partnership, and about the organization itself. I listened to my wife and my girls, who were ten and fifteen at the time, as they described how moved they were by what they saw and how they recognized the good accomplished by providing people with shoes. Listening to them, I not only realized that my family would be okay and that we would find the right time to move to Nashville together; I also realized that participating in this work would leave an indelible stamp on them that they would carry forward into other parts of their lives.

I have come to value the wisdom and expertise of people such as Sam, Raul, and Mark and Sergei, our partners in Poland/Ukraine/ Transnistria, just as I have come to value the people I have the pleasure to work with at S4S. More than twelve years after I started, I still get excited to go to work every day. I feel lucky to be part of an organization so intent on making the world a little bit better. We try to make that feeling tangible because it is key in attracting and keeping world-class talent. We have created a special place to work; but what that means today is different from what it was both in 2012 and post-pandemic, and it is changing again as I write this. Real leaders know they are never done building a great team.

I have had a lot to say about the mission and values, and the operating system and how it translates to a strong team that can tackle any challenge. All of this is true. But it has to be backed up by looking at the right now. Here are a few ways we reinforce our culture:

- We send an anonymous eNPS survey to our team every month.

- We participate in an annual "Best Not-For-Profits To Work For" survey (we made the top fifty in 2022, 2023, and 2024!), which gives us detailed feedback.

- We have skip-level meetings where I meet with each team without their supervisors at least three times a year so I can hear their concerns directly.

- We do a compensation study every twelve to twenty-four months to be sure we're still paying market salaries for comparable organizations.

- We have an all-team meeting every Monday morning at 9:30 a.m.

- We work hard so that every person in the organization can earn a bonus.

- We completely close down the last week of December and the first week of July to let the whole team recharge.

- We hire team members by using a team to screen and interview candidates.

BUILDING A STRONG TEAM

Whatever it means to get culture "right," it has to incorporate both the big things *and* the details. It's through the dozens of small decisions we make every day that we show what our culture is; what it really means to work at S4S. Like trust, culture takes years to build/earn, and it can be wiped out in minutes.

For us, it comes down to creating an environment in which everyone feels as though we're all in this together.

And that "all" certainly includes our board, as you will see next.

"STEPS" YOUR ORGANIZATION CAN TAKE

- Treat people like people—not as resources or assets. Like you, they often bring their personal lives to work and take their work lives home. This can be complicated, but it's one of the best things about being a leader. You get to shape, listen, and, if you're lucky, sometimes follow your team.

- If you need to be right all the time, you probably shouldn't be in charge of people. Good ideas come from everywhere. When you show respect and listen without ego, there's almost nothing you and your team cannot do.

- Don't assume that the "perks" of doing mission-driven work can be compensation on their own. Most of us want our work to be meaningful, but these are jobs that require talent, skill, and vision, and people should be paid accordingly.

- Thinking that diversity is some "woke" trend is shortsighted. In addition to the visible ways we can see difference, geography, age, work experience, politics, and religion are other elements that bring more perspectives to the table to help you make consistently better decisions. Whatever else you think about diversity, it's a winning strategy. If you have any doubts, look at nature's track record and spend some time exploring "hybrid vigor," or read the excellent *Team of Rivals* by Doris Kearns Goodwin.

- Mostly, work is serious—it can be demanding, and among many nonprofit organizations emotionally overwhelming—but there's joy and fun as well. Take the time to seek out and celebrate that, too. And if it's not your strong suit (it's not mine), make sure you have people who do.

- Different people find different rewards in their work. Remember that the golden rule of "Treat others as you would like to be treated" is good, but the platinum rule of "Treat others as they want to be treated" is probably better.

CHAPTER 8

Our Secret Weapon: A Committed Board

*Many receive advice,
only the wise profit from it.*

—HARPER LEE

In 2012, it wasn't just our team that felt emotionally thrashed. So did our board members. While some were more invested in S4S than others, all of them had put their reputations on the line, and now S4S's work was being called into question. Some members resigned at the first hint of trouble; some stayed on to see if they could land the plane; and some thought I couldn't turn S4S around, so they quit rather than watch it fail. I wasn't there, so I can't judge, but it seems like a cautionary tale of what can happen when the board isn't committed.

While the board absolutely had real responsibility for how bad things had gotten, they also parted ways with the founder/CEO, made other personnel changes at the top of the organization, and ran a national search for a new CEO to lead the company out of the tailspin. When the board got to three members and we started outlining the new board responsibilities, one of those three left rather than commit to even modest financial support—a basic nonprofit board member expectation.

At that point, all that was left were the two board members who had helped found S4S, and they were tired. During the interview process, I shared with them that I saw an engaged board as key to S4S's success. So, after the first six months, and with their support, we began to rebuild what I think of today as our secret strategic advantage: a world-class board.

Not every company or organization is required to have a board. Publicly traded companies and nonprofits do, but given how many other companies are out there, the vast majority do not. And I think this is a *huge* missed opportunity. I have served on the boards of three private for-profit companies, and I know (because they told me!) how much value they gained from having an outside perspective. We sold two of those companies for very fair prices. Each owner said this would not have been possible without an outside board, and those transactions generated generational wealth for their families.

THE NATURE OF BOARDS

These might be rare examples, but I believe every organization and business would benefit from a committed, engaged board. Board members can provide invaluable oversight, open doors, and question assumptions that you might not even know you're making. Whether it's seeing an opportunity or avoiding a loss, good boards provide real wisdom to guide the strategy and decision-making process.

In the nonprofit space, boards usually have two legal responsibilities: 1) to hire/fire/evaluate the CEO, and 2) to ensure the organization's fiscal health. Neither of these responsibilities should be taken lightly, but the best boards do far more. For S4S, our board members are advisors and partners in generating the resources the organization needs to achieve its mission. They stress test strategy with the management team. They are a check and balance to make sure we are good stewards of the money, shoes, clothes, and time that thousands of people entrust to us. They are volunteer ambassadors who care about making a difference and are willing to invest their own time, treasure, and talent to the cause. In short, they are remarkable.

A nonprofit board such as ours and a for-profit board are more similar than many people realize. The board has the same two top concerns: the CEO relationship, and doing what's right for the financial health of the company (what for-profit boards call "creating shareholder value"). Board members (usually) remain outside the business, but they have to put in time to understand the company, its markets, its people, and its strategy. If you replace "shareholder" with "mission" in the board's duty to exercise care, obedience, and loyalty, you get essentially the same set of standards for a nonprofit board.

Our board members evaluate the methodologies for reaching organizational milestones, but they also put their reputations on the line as they make introductions to potential donors or partners, opening doors for growth and investment. If you are an S4S board member, you're involved in a way that a for-profit member is likely to never be, literally going into the field to put shoes on someone's feet, or giving someone in need a winter coat, or participating in a shoe drive. The time commitment is high, and, in our case, there is an expectation that you will help to bring in cash, product, and in-kind services, or make introductions.

 ANOTHER VOICE | Clay Jenkins

Prior to creating Clay Jenkins Collective, Clay was the senior vice president of worldwide sourcing for Caleres, a $2.6 billion global footwear company. His role included factory compliance and social responsibility, supplier relationships, technical services, and new business development. He is an emeritus board member of Soles4Souls.

Evolution

When Buddy asked me to consider joining the board, like everyone in the industry, I was aware of the negative press the organization had received, and because I was at the director level at Caleres, before I accepted, I approached our CEO Diane Sullivan. We had donated to S4S on its very first disaster relief project, and Diane's response was, "I've always believed in the mission. Take the board position. The only thing I'm going to ask is that you just check in with me and let me know how you think it's going. We trust you. Go get involved."

When I attended the first few board meetings, it was a bit of a shock. There were something like six of us in the room, including Buddy, and we encountered an organization that was struggling to make payroll. Buddy faced one challenge after another. He only had a handful of team members remaining, including David Graben, who I came to love. I respected David's passion and commitment, even if he was a dreamer and sometimes his ideas could be hard to follow.

In those early days, Buddy brought in excellent new board members who had high levels of professional experience and came from lots of different industries, which was a huge benefit. We had members from Fortune 1000 companies, logistics experts, and people with finance backgrounds, and our board chair Bernadette Lane had a career in nonprofits and fundraising. She was the voice of reason for all of us on the board who didn't know anything about nonprofit. We did know business, and our collective corporate business knowledge increased the organization's professionalism and allowed us to refine strategy and bring more focus.

Over my time, the board undertook a clear evolution that included diversifying the board by industry and background. Bernard Turner was one of the first board members in that nucleus during my time. He was a professor of social enterprise at Belmont University. He was appropriately critical of the lack of board diversity, often saying, "We're serving people of color and I'm the only one that's of color, and I'm a professor." S4S has benefited from diversifying the board, and now it is far more reflective of the people S4S serves internationally and domestically, particularly in the 4Opportunity program where a majority of the entrepreneurs are women.

S4S grew in another sense with the acquisition of Dignity U Wear, making the sensible decision to retain its advisory council, made up of footwear and apparel industry experts. Not only have some of those individuals joined the board; the continuation of the council has deepened corporate ties. Buddy also had the vision to draw on the experience of its members and create a "board buddy" program where experienced members mentor new board recruits. They have also, wisely, formed a board emeriti group so that S4S does not lose the institutional knowledge of past board members.

One of the early turning points of the board's evolution was the suggestion by Bernadette Lane for the board of directors to travel internationally to a country S4S has served. We held the first meeting in Haiti. Nothing like spending three days together on buses, in meetings, and over bag lunches and dinner to strengthen relationships. That trip galvanized us as a board to understand the work and embrace the mission. The practice continues to this day.

The results of such evolution are revealing because now people raise their hands and want to be a part of something so

> professional that accomplishes so much good. There was a lot of hard work in those early years, but those reports back to Diane Sullivan were always about an organization that was improving and serving more people.

GROWING THE S4S BOARD

Based on my experience at the YPO, I entered S4S believing that having an independent board was critically important, and that good governance was table stakes. While that was the right thing to say, convincing new people to join the board was a huge lift because transparency demanded they knew what they were getting into. The work would be worth it, but being on the S4S board in 2013 was hard. Hard is not impossible, of course, and the vision of creating a legitimate board with experienced, visionary leaders received a huge jump start when Bernadette Lane joined. Bernadette was a credible and distinguished executive, an expert at fundraising, and well-versed in international nonprofits. Just as you need proof of concept to bring a new product to market, adding Bernadette gave us social proof—if she had vetted S4S, then others would feel more confident in joining. Most potential board members come through connections they share with our team or other board members, not through me. Although I was deeply involved in recruiting prospective members, we had to cast a wide net to find prospects who had the stature and expertise we needed. From the outset, we succeeded in attracting excellent board members, and now the board is recruiting members themselves, which further accelerates our ability to find amazing people who want to serve. Beginning in 2016, new board members joined with the knowledge that there was an expectation that they would be financially involved and central to sharing the S4S story among

OUR SECRET WEAPON: A COMMITTED BOARD

potential donors, partners, and industry insiders. There was clarity about their responsibilities and their obligations. Their engagement continues to make a huge difference to our trajectory.

Initially, we did not ask prospective board members to donate or to be responsible for raising money. Make no mistake, we needed donors, but we hadn't earned that right yet. Bernadette was soon joined by Clay Jenkins, who was senior vice president with Caleres, a company you will recognize through some of their brands, including Famous Footwear, Sam Edelman, Naturalizer, Allen Edmonds, Vionic, and Dr. Scholl's Shoes. I met Clay when I was in St. Louis to visit with other Caleres executives, and when Clay heard I was in town, he reached out and wanted to have lunch. He initially made a donation as an individual, but when I shared that we were rebuilding the board and told him that Pat McLaughlin, a well-known footwear CEO, had joined, Clay agreed to come on board. Soon we met our short-term goal of expanding the board to twelve members from our low point of three. Today, we have twenty-two members, and we stay fully engaged with our emeritus members such that they can continue to stay involved with S4S as much as they choose.

We've continued to get better and better in how we approach prospective board members, largely because of the wise counsel of their predecessors. Now, we have a prospective board member packet that lays out everything from the meeting schedule to the financials to committee makeup. Board members can serve two, three-year terms. They are expected to serve on at least one committee, and most people are on two. We have four board calls per year and two in-person meetings. Typically, one of the in-person meetings is held in the US, and the other is somewhere we have 4Opportunity partners. Our goal is to get board members to directly experience the work S4S does on a daily basis, whether that's by visiting our main distribution center in Alabama or going abroad where they engage with 4Opportunity partners, communities, and customers in places such as Haiti, Honduras, Guatemala, and the Dominican Republic. They participate in the extraordinarily moving act of providing new shoes to people in need and feeling the connection in that moment. We use these board meetings to create engagement that shifts their experience from an intellectual exercise to an emotional reality.

One of their commitments is financial—something we are fully transparent about. At present, our expectation is that members generate $100,000 in economic impact. We share, of course, that there are lots of ways a director can reach that goal, including donating product, collecting shoes, providing in-kind services, and through establishing connections or introducing potential corporate partners and/or funders. We also expect each board member to make a meaningful personal financial contribution. At the end of June 2024, we had 100% of our directors hit that target.

We want to create the means to say "yes" as much as we can in service of our mission. For example, Stacy Xie, then at the consulting firm AlixPartners, assisted us in exploring some new business ideas. She provided her own expertise and brought in a couple of her team members, forming a knowledge base that, had we paid for it out of pocket, would certainly have cost at least $75,000. Steve Reynolds, another board member, has been involved with The Clinton Global Initiative for decades. He was able to secure us two tickets to their annual summit—tickets that sell for $5,000 a piece—and the benefit from attending the summit in knowledge gained, inspiration, and networking was absolutely worth more than the $10,000 in economic impact.

MAINTAINING AN EXCELLENT BOARD

We have continually looked for ways to improve and diversify our board so that we can access different perspectives, experiences, and expertise. We have maintained the participation of board members from within the footwear and apparel industries, and we have augmented those from the retail, finance, and consulting sectors, among others. We have had success recruiting members with meaningful nonprofit and international experience. We now have an even mix of women and men, and we try to maintain racial and geographic diversity. This intentionality has not gone unnoticed by our partners on the ground. I experienced a proud moment during our July 2024 board meeting, which we hosted in the Dominican Republic. Sam Darguin, our longtime 4Opportunity partner and director of the HAC, said to the entire group, "I've seen how you guys have changed. You are different and you look different. And just so you know, it matters to us to see ourselves at that table."

That's been a transformation—from being effective at showing up in moments of crisis with free shoes (something we continue to do) to having a sustained presence in improving a place's economic opportunity through committed partners, like Sam, who are deeply invested in their communities for the long haul. Those board members who came on in the early years of our transformation, many of whom arrived around the same time, created a unique bond because of the depth of their involvement and the amount of work required of them to help us turn the organization around. Some were worried that, without the sense of ownership that they felt, the energy they generated because of that bonding would not be sustainable among new members. That fear hasn't been realized. Today's board members' connection is different from theirs, no doubt, but we have been able to sustain passion for the mission. Because we have been purposeful in creating overlap in the board terms, we have shaped opportunities for new members to learn from those who have previous experience. We are always looking for new people, and that constant infusion of fresh ideas has been one of the ways the board has continued to strengthen. Age diversity is sometimes overlooked. But our most recent board chair, Aaron Bellville, who first arrived as a board intern through a Nashville program called Young Leaders Council that places young professionals on nonprofit boards, is an example of why that matters.

ANOTHER VOICE | **Aaron Belville**

Aaron Belville leads Banfield Pet Hospital's People and Organization function, where he and his team focus on creating programs and resources for Banfield's eighteen thousand associates nationwide. He holds a bachelor's degree from Lipscomb University, a law degree from the University of Tennessee, and an MBA from Ole Miss. He is an emeritus board chair for Soles4Souls.

Legacy and Expansion

I first started volunteering with Soles4Souls as a board intern and never dreamed at the time that one day I would be its chair. I fell in love with the organization quickly. I found it to be so focused on impact, which was refreshing because, unfortunately, there are a lot of nonprofits that do more talking than doing. I joined at a time when the organization had stabilized and was soon looking to grow with the expansion into 4EveryKid—and if you want to talk about a pretty tall task, getting to every homeless child in America certainly meets that definition. There were still a few board members who had been through the tough times and did the hard work to get S4S back on the rails. The rest of us benefited from their

> hard work. Their edict had been different from ours. We had the benefit of what they and the leadership team had accomplished, and that allowed us to focus on growth and extending our mission.
>
> Here's an example of how far S4S had evolved. When I first started attending board meetings, they kept talking about this thing called the "squirrel account," and I'm thinking, *What the heck is the squirrel account?* "That's where we squirrel away money to make sure we can float payroll and other recurring expenses period over period." Just a few years later, under Milledge Hart's guidance, S4S was able to create an innovation fund where we have been able to "squirrel away" several hundred thousand dollars, exclusively for forward-looking innovation. It was this interest-bearing fund that allowed the leadership team to seek out consulting expertise as we developed the 4EveryKid program. If we hadn't had that flexibility, the initiative probably wouldn't have been possible. Talk about evolution. In twenty years, S4S has gone from being a disaster relief agency to becoming a revenue generator through its international programming, to developing the capacity and expertise to both raise the necessary capital and reach public school children in every part of the country. Most organizations couldn't make that evolution over the course of fifty years.

Often, there are mutual benefits realized by having engaged board members. We have two board members who are on the operations and sourcing side of the footwear and apparel industry. Aaron Lord is vice president, supply chain planning for Capri Holdings, and Dan Friedman is the chief sourcing officer for Caleres. Because our 4EveryKid program is far more logistically intensive than anything S4S has done before, they worked with Mike Shirey, our COO, and together they have sought to maximize efficiency in our warehouses to support the program. We have five warehouses in the US, one in Canada, and one in the Netherlands. These two board members have brought their logistics expertise to the table pro bono, including providing additional people within their companies to give us guidance. AlixPartners came back with another deep dive into how to optimize our warehouse network that we would likely never have been able to afford. They believe in our mission and the 4EveryKid program and want to see the program succeed. At the same time, the interaction also allows them to meet other people in the industry and expand their networks, which is an unquantifiable benefit to them and to us.

One of the things I most respect about our board is that they have adopted our values as their own. They support one another and hold each other accountable, right down to meeting attendance and their impact numbers. Twice a year, board members get a report on their economic impact and engagement. We have an expectation that all members attend 80% of the meetings. If someone falls below the line, the board chair has a conversation with them. No one slips by. Every eighteen months, the board completes a self-evaluation through an industry standard survey so they can benchmark themselves against other nonprofits by size and number of employees. The results are a road map for how to continue improving the board's performance and experience.

Board members also serve on at least one of the seven board committees: programs, finance/audit, business development, fundraising, marketing/communications, governance, and the executive committee. They respect their role, but they can also flex up when circumstances warrant. For example, when our CFO Robert Adams-Ghee died unexpectedly, we hired an interim CFO. He did a remarkable job, but there was no way he could have deep organizational knowledge immediately, so the finance committee was able to provide insight and context, guiding him by asking the right questions.

Robert's death also prompted a frank discussion with the executive committee about succession planning, including highly transparent conversations that require incredibly high levels of trust and respect—exactly why an effective board is indispensable.

Our board members are excellent at maintaining their advisory involvement with the organization without overstepping. The nature of our board demonstrates each member's commitment and showcases them as stewards of the work we do collectively. And, just as with our leadership team, when board members demonstrate that they act upon our core values, this has a trickle-down effect on our team.

ANOTHER VOICE | **Bernadette Lane**

Emeritus Board Chair

Thinking Forward

The caliber of the board that Soles4Souls has recruited over the years just keeps going up and up, and certainly other board members have a lot to do with that, but so has the steady hand of leadership. It is a board and leadership team that has tremendous credibility that is attractive to those considering joining it.

I think this was reflected when S4S established the board emeriti. Its function demonstrates their core values, because emeriti members have all the same privileges as standing board members, with the exception of voting rights. As a member of the board emeriti, I am invited to all of the meetings, and I can be as involved as I want or am able. This enables a person to stay connected and informed and aware, which is unusual and allows the organization to sustain some of the knowledge and experience of those of us who have served. It's a great example of forward thinking.

THE POWER OF PERSPECTIVE

Our board members always maintain a clear sense that they are partners in helping us achieve the larger objectives of the organization. They bring their expertise to our leadership team but do so without agenda or ego. These qualities were on display when we were pursuing an acquisition that I thought would expand our sustainability capacity, diversify our revenue streams, and help us access new products to serve more people. The board, which included several members experienced in mergers and acquisitions, never pushed a position during our discussions. Instead, they asked questions, counseled me on best practices to analyze the risk and opportunity, and assisted our team in examining the market potential. We had access to advisory experience that would have cost us hundreds of thousands of dollars. Instead, we received specific, relevant, informed advice ... for free. I really wanted to do this deal. In the end, by considering their questions in the spirit given, we decided the upside was not worth the risk. Collectively, we reached the right decision in the right way. They shared their experiences but never said "no." Instead, they said, "This is a management decision," allowing us the autonomy to reach our decision as a leadership team. They played their role beautifully. Our management team did so as well, pushing when appropriate, responding as needed, and together reaching the decision that the acquisition was the wrong thing for that moment.

This spirit extends to the board's central role of assessing the one person who reports to them directly: Me. Every year, when I receive my annual performance review, they show me the positive things I have accomplished and areas that need improvement. It's respectful and candid, neither a love fest nor an interrogation. I don't want to paint a picture that every review is sweetness and light. I'm human and so are our board members. There are parts of any annual performance review that leave me mad, scratching my head, or most often looking in the mirror. That's as it should be. I cannot get better if I don't face the things that need attention.

ANOTHER VOICE | **Angela Harrell**

Angela Harrell joined Voya Financial in 2014 and serves as senior vice president, chief diversity and corporate impact officer, and president, Voya Foundation. She is the board chair of Soles4Souls.

I Speak in "We"

I speak in "we" when I refer to the work that Soles4Souls does. It's how I feel about the organization. My love affair with S4S started when I first arrived at Voya ten years ago. We had S4S shoe collection boxes in the hallway at our office, and I'd bring in my stuff. I hate waste. I love the idea of things having a second life and making a difference for folks in some way, even if it's small. That's how it started. My participation with S4S grew exponentially as I learned more about them, ultimately landing me on the board.

Nonprofit boards often don't function as for-profit boards in the way they are structured or how they act upon their governance role. That is not the case at S4S. Here, there are no perfunctory "Here are the financials" calls for a rubber stamp. If a leadership team relies on a board only as a mechanism to report on everything they are doing, they are not benefiting from the expertise of everyone seated in the room. One of the reasons why I think S4S has such high-caliber board directors and long board tenure is because we have engaging, robust conversations around complex, sophisticated, purpose-oriented endeavors and initiatives. The essentials of people's lives are better enabled through what we do. It's an awesome responsibility and a privilege to serve. The high caliber of my fellow board directors means that while I lend my time and expertise to S4S, I grow as a professional and as an individual because I learn from humanitarians who are also titans of industry. I'm being served while I am serving, and that's really something special.

Another thing that is unique to S4S is that we don't have committees for the sake of having committees. Some nonprofits don't have board committees, or the remit is very limited in scope. At S4S, our committees have a real strategic priority. Every committee has a chair who is a board director and their co-lead is a member of the S4S leadership team. We get things done. Every committee has a specific role and agenda that is substantive. A lot of what we do is "pressure testing." What a board is meant to do is ask questions, give input, provide perspective, but not develop or even execute on strategy. What we bring to bear is all of the expertise that we've had as business and nonprofit leaders to help leadership think ahead, look around corners, and take into consideration the economic, social, and political factors that may influence their growth strategy and all of the milestones along the way.

Maintaining a focus on being agile, flexible, and nimble is key to growing and sustaining an organization. This focus is foundational to what you develop within people, within leaders, and within systems, so that as things shift and change, you have the foresight and ability to change the actions that you take. You don't change what you know, but you change how you apply it and when. All strong organizations have this built into their fabric.

It's easy to be a part of something that is so well-run, so well-organized, led by people with not just the science. The science is important, but there has to be a marriage of science and humanity. At S4S, I can pour into our mission to disrupt the cycle of poverty and, in the process, also get my own cup filled.

A DIFFERENT LEVEL OF INVOLVEMENT

Successful engagement from a board starts with the members' passion for the mission. It grows by their involvement. Board members can have a slightly arm's-length perspective that is not tangled up in the daily management of people and processes. A highly engaged, high-functioning board is the best advantage a leadership team can have. And the quickest path to forming such a board is being thoughtful about who joins it and remaining clear about its purpose.

Let me close this chapter with one last example of board engagement. This one is entirely unique to our organization, but it reflects our values and the culture we want to create. It focuses on one last requirement we ask of our board members—a requirement initiated by our current board chair, Angela Harrell. She conceived of the idea to ask all the board members to collect at least a hundred pairs of shoes. Just like any one of our donors—from kindergarteners to CEOs—this request has our board members turning to connections from their workplaces, their churches, their kids' schools, personal networks, you name it. Here's the simple reality: Holding a shoe drive, especially a very modest one like this, is easy to talk about until a hundred pairs of smelly shoes show up in your house. As a board member works to secure a hundred pairs of shoes directly from people they know, it puts the process into useful perspective as they turn to a board report about someone who spearheaded a shoe drive that generated twenty-five thousand pairs. When board members experience loading a hundred pair of shoes into their trunk one day and bookend that with meeting an entrepreneur who has helped her family out of poverty in a tiny village in a faraway country another day, the full circle of our work comes home. We probably all believe that we can imagine what a hundred pairs of shoes looks like ... until you put them in the back of your car. And when a board member looks at their trunk and remembers that S4S needs to collect five million pairs of shoes every year and differentiate those that are usable from those that are not, a lasting reality sets in.

Now, you probably won't have your board members fill their car trunks with shoes. But you definitely need them to understand both the "why" and the "how" of what you do with that level of connection and understanding. Your mission is a constant, but the means to get there and the problems encountered along the way, are forever changing. All organizations must be dynamic because the world is a dynamic place. Change is particularly difficult to manage at key inflection points of crisis or growth. An engaged board gives you additional tools to navigate change.

The best, brightest CEOs are made brighter by having engaged boards advising them. Smart CEOs recognize this. They come to see their board as a vital partner—a word I will expand on in the next chapter.

"STEPS" YOUR ORGANIZATION CAN TAKE

- Surround yourself with smart people. Who wouldn't want to have ten, or fifteen, or twenty really smart people present at their side as they try to solve problems?

- Seek diversity—in background, gender, race, age, expertise, and industry. Diverse minds strengthen a board. You can access a wider knowledge base and gain perspectives otherwise not available to you. The traditional "old boys' networks" miss too much. The board is supposed to make you better, not make you feel better.

- Be honest with yourself. Having an engaged board requires the CEO to be self-aware in order to hear the hard stuff. Good boards tell the truth.

- Leverage them. Engaged board members are some of the best ambassadors you'll ever have.

- Recruit from their networks. Your great board members today will help you attract great board members for tomorrow.

CHAPTER 9

Cultivating Great Partnerships

*Alone we can do so little;
together we can do so much.*
—HELEN KELLER

At S4S, partnership is so central to how we think that we are probably guilty of overusing the word. I know new employees often wonder who is *not* a partner! It might be confusing, but it is central to understanding how we work. In other organizations, I suspect many people view partnerships as transactional—a relationship defined by "If you do this, then I do that," rather than "I will do this regardless." S4S thinks differently. Often, we have no contracts. We might have a "memorandum of understanding," usually to spell out any restrictions on where shoes and clothes can go or the cost of logistics. For us, real partnership is about the work we accomplish together. I understand that our broad definition wouldn't work for a lot of organizations, but in our case, I wouldn't want to do anything that made us stop thinking about everybody in our ecosystem as a partner.

That said, obviously not *everybody* is a partner. The companies that provide us with electricity or internet services are not "partners" for us any more than they are for you. But in our particular ecosystem, nearly everyone else is. They include corporate donors, individuals, foundations, NGOs and philanthropic organizations, social enterprises, and wholesale distributors.

In the broadest sense, these partnerships fall into two main groups:

1. Those that are about resources coming into S4S: product and financial donations. These are literally the raw materials that we use to create opportunities for people.

2. Those that are about creating the impact on the ground. These are the people and organizations that get those products into the hands (or onto the feet) of the people who directly benefit.

We turn to partners because we need their help, but we want to be a partner who helps them accomplish a mission or solve a problem as well. We also want to develop partnerships for the long term—indeed, several of our partnerships (of every kind) date back to the beginnings of S4S. Cultivating partnerships takes time and effort. Great partnerships have their seeds in good relationships, and good relationships are built on respect and trust.

Knowing that and acting on it isn't always as easy as it sounds. I'm not proud to admit that there was a time in our history when S4S wasn't consistently a good partner. Of course, that was never our intention, but there were instances when we did not have the finances, logistics, or scale to deliver on our promises. One instance when we failed still sticks in my mind ten years later.

In 2014, we were anxious to seize an opportunity to form a 4Opportunity partnership in the Philippines. David Graben found a potential nonprofit, Seeds of Dignity, which had a program focused on income-generating opportunities and an entrepreneurial mindset. Check. David arrived in the country as the first shipment was delivered, and he returned on fire with stories of how people instantly got the model and were selling shoes on day one. One enterprising young man set up outside a nursing school where the students had a little more disposable income. He sold out almost immediately; but rather than closing shop, he started collecting mobile numbers so he could let his customers know when the next shipment arrived. We couldn't tell that story fast enough!

But the story didn't end there, unfortunately. We were still coming out of our tailspin, and we didn't yet have the donation volume to consistently deliver product. When it came time for the second shipment, the cupboard was empty. The response from our new partner was predictable, accurate, and brutal. He told us, "You came here and you showed me what was possible and then broke your promise. What am I supposed to tell these people after you raised their hopes? You not only failed me; you failed them." Not many people at S4S remember that story, but I think about it every time we go into another country and tell someone that we want to be partners. We hurt the guy we'd made commitments to, and we hurt the people who were counting on him. To be a trustworthy partner you not only have to be able to deliver on your promises in the moment; you have to ask yourself, can I be here for them in five years? Ten years? Livelihoods and futures are at stake.

We have been on the other side of disappointment, too. Until a few years ago, we had a phenomenal national retail partner. They'd created a "buy one, give one" program: For every winter coat a customer bought, our partner donated one—and we were able to place these coats directly onto the backs of people in need here in the US. They had been clear with us from the start that they would run the campaign once a year, and there wasn't appetite for a larger partnership or any additional requests. While the program did tremendous good and we remain grateful for the quality and volume of their donations, they saw the program mainly as promotional. We like partnerships that run deeper and create more opportunities for everyone in the ecosystem. Still, we were getting winter coats to people who needed them. The retailer ended up running the program for ten years, providing over 200,000 coats! But success created a different problem. Along with our distribution partners in schools, homeless shelters, and domestic violence programs, we had gotten used to the annual availability of these great coats. When it ended, there was a big gap in our ability to serve them. We continue to receive calls from the nonprofit agencies who had delivered coats to those in need. Each time we get a call, it's a tough thing to say that they are no longer available. Our partnership with that retailer had a huge impact, and we still regret that it isn't one that we have been able to sustain.

While that partnership was an example of a huge impact but without a deep connection, I'd also like to share a few that illustrate how much more can be done when those things come together.

CORPORATE PARTNERS

It might seem disingenuous, even cynical, to call a donor a partner, sort of like saying someone who makes a charitable donation is an "investor." It's a legitimate question, if we're just trying to make everyone feel better. The donors, whether donating products or money, aren't getting a return in the traditional sense. But it's a missed opportunity to understand the nuances of giving if we don't acknowledge the benefits that go both ways. The best relationships we have with our corporate partners are those where we can help them solve a business problem. Part of that problem might be employee engagement, or the CEO wanting to give back to the communities where they live and work. Another part might be around hitting their sustainability goals.

It might just be that they need to free up some warehouse space. But if we only focus on their philanthropy, we miss the opportunity to go deeper and form lasting relationships.

Partnership is not only the best strategy; it's our only option! Because, while a really organized and supported shoe drive might produce tens of thousands of shoes, even a wildly successful one is never going to produce 250,000 items of new product the way a corporate partner can. Our impact would be a fraction of what it is without corporate partners. If we can help them spread the news about the good work they are doing while helping them solve a problem at the same time, it can be a win for everyone. That's a partnership.

 ANOTHER VOICE | **Nancy Youssef**

Chief business development officer and executive vice president, International, Soles4Souls

Full Circle

When Soles4Souls is placing corporate donated product around the world, we have to be gritty and think about both being a nonprofit that is doing good *and* how we can be commercially viable for our corporate partners. From their perspective, their interests aren't solely focused on doing good—they're also influenced by factors such as market trends, political events, or cultural shifts shaping their decisions. It's important for us to understand what aligns with their priorities while considering what's beneficial for us as well. The goal is to create a mutually beneficial dynamic that fosters long-term partnerships that both sides are motivated to sustain.

To do that, we've got to be accountable. If we say we're going to do something, we do that something, and then we report back on how we did it. If we make a mistake, we've got to make it right. We'll go back and say, "Okay, here's what happened and here's how we are going to keep it from happening again." We take accountability seriously, but we also try to remind ourselves and our partners that, at the end of the day, what's most important is how meaningful the work is. Where are their donations going? Whose body and whose feet did the items end up on? We share how their donation has impacted lives. Who is that one human being who received those shoes or that shirt? That's what it all comes back to.

DSW: A CASE STUDY OF GREAT CORPORATE PARTNERSHIP

Corporate partnerships are demanding for the retailers, not just because of costs and complex logistics but because they requires significant training and support for frontline workers. Big companies can have a huge impact, and we have certainly had many partners who are in it for the long haul, who are as focused on impact as we are. DSW is a great example. Over the seven years the company has collected donated shoes in its stores, it has invested beyond the cardboard collection boxes we used to supply to new, branded, attractive, durable bins that it places in visible locations near the front of its stores. An even larger investment comes in the time, energy, and expertise DSW has put into educating its team members about the nature of our work and mission. It has also made a huge investment in covering one of the most expensive parts of our business: shipping. DSW covers the costs from its stores to our distribution centers because millions of pairs of donated shoes mean little if we can't get them to the end user. When the cost of shipping shoes from all DSW's stores to our Alabama warehouse was rising, putting the whole program at risk, both of us got creative. We simply don't have the financial wherewithal to cover the costs of getting shoes from thousands of retail stores to a sorting and distribution facility. However, because we have a number of regional warehouses, the operations team, working side-by-side with DSW logistics and IT leaders, figured out how to cut the shipping costs in half. We value our partners and want to help create the means for them to remain partners.

A good portion of our durable partnership has been formed because DSW has supported an employee travel program, which allows coworkers to nominate one another to join our trips to visit direct partners. We probably take fifty DSW employees a year on our travel programs so they can experience the impact of donations firsthand. They come back and share stories, which is a thousand times more powerful than the best corporate video DSW could ever produce. They experience how the shoes bring joy to people and meet the entrepreneurs whose lives are changed. And because these entrepreneurs are overwhelmingly women—just like 70% of the DSW customer base—the connection clicks. Their participation can be life-changing. I will never forget a part-time, teenage DSW employee from Canada who joined an S4S trip to Guatemala. She had never traveled outside of Canada, had never been on a plane. She returned home a changed person. She will remember her trip for the rest of her life, thanks to an employer who sees philanthropy as so much more than good public relations.

Our partnership with DSW reveals so many elements of what it takes to build a sustainable and meaningful relationship: operations, marketing, employee engagement, shared mission. It's a rich example of a long-term, deep partnership.

ANOTHER VOICE | Amy Jo Donohew

Amy Jo Donohew is chief human resources officer and senior vice president at Designer Brands, the parent company of DSW.

Making It Personal

The Designer Brands/DSW relationship with Soles4Souls started in 2018, and while the majority of the interaction then was under the purview of our marketing team, I had adjacency because I oversaw all of our associate relations, and that meant making certain our store associates understood what Soles4Souls was, how it operated, and how we supported it. It takes both prioritization and education on our partnership and how it works for our associates to become good ambassadors for the program. At DSW, we recognize that customers want to spend their money where they feel businesses are doing good things and giving back. There is an absolute proven ROI when your customer knows what you're doing when it comes to philanthropy and sustainability. More than that, they want to support such work. I knew that our associates' knowledge of S4S would be key to leveraging customers' desire to bring materials into our stores to donate.

The relationship with S4S was unique not only in its entrepreneurial model, which offered us a very different way of thinking about giving back, but they had also taken engagement much further by making it possible for our associates to join international trips to experience the 4Opportunity program in action. When COVID-19 came along, not only did those trips stop, but the impact on the retail environment was substantial and required that DSW pause some of its giving and eliminate several roles. When we restarted charitable programming in 2021, I volunteered to oversee this and bring it fully into the HR world. Beyond providing a different kind of model through its international entrepreneur support, S4S was also refreshingly different from many organizations because its leadership team recognizes that we're running a for-profit business and acknowledges what that means in a very meaningful way. S4S understands that, to be our effective partner, it needs to see how it fits into our business strategy. In order to maximize our ROI through the partnership, we've connected it to our customer loyalty program. For example, customers receive loyalty points when they come into the store to donate shoes and can then apply those points to purchases. If customers have points left over at the end of the year, they can use those points to donate shoes online where their points are translated into dollars that DSW then sends to S4S. In 2023, we took our philanthropic participation a step further through a foundation DSW has established, which has included "register roundups" (rounding up purchases to an even dollar amount) on behalf of S4S during specific campaign timeframes such as the back-to-school and holiday seasons. This has allowed us to drive over $2 million in cash donations to S4S in addition to the ten million pairs of shoes we have helped orchestrate over the last six years.

This deepening of our relationship with S4S and the corresponding growth in our donations is fueled by two things. First, it's the payoff from training and participation in its travel programs that has educated our associates on both the organization's "why" and "how." Informed associate engagement with customers has, in turn, had a measurable impact on our ability to acquire new customers and to improve our attachment rate, vital in an era when store traffic is declining and sales conversion on store visitations matters immensely. Second, in 2023, we worked with S4S to coordinate a trip for our executive retail team to Honduras. That immersion was a game changer because our team had firsthand experience seeing the impact the creation of sustainable income has had there. They became emotionally invested in the work in a manner that has trickled down into their teams to make this more of a priority than it's ever been. Where it used to be that the participation in donations and the knowledge base of associates varied widely store to store, these two approaches have created consistency across the company.

I'm not surprised at these outcomes because I've experienced them myself. After my husband and I went on our first Honduran trip, I came home ready to quit my job, throw off all trappings of the material world, and open our own nonprofit to save the world. Once I calmed down and suffered a mix of some humoring and some sympathetic support from my husband, I realized I could make the biggest impact on helping people through this corporate partnership DSW had established with S4S. I could drive this initiative and use my position to maximize our impact—my own little piece of bettering the world. The mission of S4S has really become a big part of who I am and a big part of DSW.

UNIQUE PARTNERSHIP MODELS

Whether it's with DSW, or with other amazing companies such as Zappos, Deckers Brands (which owns UGG and Hoka), or Brooks, I'm burying the lede if I only talk about how we solve a business problem for them. Because the truth is, lots of for-profit companies can do that. *But*, what they can't usually do is help them tell a meaningful story—a story that gets to the "why" of our partnership, not just the outcomes.

Here's an example of what I mean. Luxury brands have some of the same issues as any brand and retailer: returns, damaged goods, excess inventory. And it's even trickier for those brands to manage such challenges in ways that don't negatively impact their market position.

We had worked with one high-end brand a few times, and unexpectedly, they had a sizeable donation. They don't see their products as a good fit with our 4Opportunity program, and a lot of their product is not really right for disaster response. With all these challenges to reconcile, we were stumped. Then our team, because of their deep understanding of the 4EveryKid ecosystem, came up with a beautiful idea. In addition to serving the kids, what if we served teachers and school administrators with this new product? I don't love sports analogies, but it was a grand slam homerun. The brand loved the idea of delighting these teachers, recognizing all the hard work they do. It was a grassroots way to involve their employees in distribution events. We deepened our partnerships with the schools because we thought about everyone who serves kids. And we were able to turn a problem into a celebration. That's an edge I think S4S has, as a not-for-profit, because we have a practical and special way to not only solve the problem, but make it a benefit for all involved. Maybe not the most obvious solution, but one that took advantage of the constraints to find a better way forward. I love it when that happens!

The models of partnership we employ at S4S are unique because we are entrepreneurial by nature, and so are our corporate partners. We each bring strengths and blind spots to these conversations. When it's transactional, there's usually little interest in or time spent on what's possible. But when that openness is a starting point, our partners' market knowledge of products and customers, combined with our ability to connect with a different way of thinking about both, can take us in surprising directions.

ANOTHER VOICE | **Tauna Dean**

Tauna Dean is the founder and owner of Kind World Collective, a recruitment and consulting firm that matches mission-driven companies with purpose-driven talent and a focus on contributing to a kinder, cleaner, and more connected world. She is a former board member of Soles4Souls.

Come as You Are

I began interacting with Soles4Souls when I was working for adidas, building its very first North American social impact team. I had just stepped into that role after several years with adidas in Germany, doing talent acquisition and executive recruiting, and I was evaluating these kinds of legacy relationships, including S4S. There wasn't much happening with that relationship at the time, so I reached out to David and Buddy, and we started to kind of think about how adidas might get product to S4S while also engaging our employees. What I had realized almost immediately at adidas was that we didn't have to create a culture of purpose; we just had to uncover it—employees really cared. Because of the programs S4S was already running, I saw that we had an opportunity for our employees to get on the ground level and see how a simple pair of shoes could impact a child in an impoverished country. I loved the idea of having our employees participate in work where they were able to experience the life cycle of a shoe and see what it could do when it gets in the right hands.

It was through this relationship that we came to know one another, and that eventually led to Buddy offering me an invitation to join the S4S board. The invitation came at an incredibly demanding time in my life, both professionally and personally—so

> demanding that I felt I wasn't contributing as much to the board as I should. When I voiced my concerns, Buddy and the team basically said, "Tauna, we know where you are in your life, and we want you here. Come as you are. We like your energy. We like who you are. We really feel like we can learn from you and vice versa." That welcoming spirit is so true to the organization and the culture it has created.
>
> Because of Kind World Creative, S4S has also turned to me to assist with recruiting, and working with its team repeated my experience of its culture that I had encountered as a board member. One of the things that I think was consistent between that experience as a board member and the one working to help the organization hire for its own team is that there's no ego, no politics. Instead, there is an altruism to the humans who are doing the work and the humans who they're supporting, which is something you feel palpably when you are among the team. S4S is unique in its consistent message: "We see you and we value you." That is a rare and wonderful dynamic that's worth celebrating.

Take adidas, for example. Like most shoe brands, it has sales representatives scattered in markets across the US. Adidas tries to be as efficient as possible by sending each sales rep one shoe—you get the right shoe in LA; I get the left shoe in Nashville. What happens at the end of the season? What do you do with one shoe? And what if you work for a company that cares enough about the environment that it doesn't want these unmatched shoes getting shipped to a facility where they will be run through a shredder? Or just stacked up in the salesperson's garage? You send them to us. We lay those shoes out in the back of our warehouse and match them up like a card game. It might take two years to find a match. While these are shoes that have never been worn, by themselves, they're almost trash. Paired, they can be used in all kinds of programs. And it keeps several members of the warehouse team in Alabama employed. All of this came from mashing up adidas's desire to reduce landfill waste, a willingness to partner creatively, and our knowledge of how to make the work pay off.

One other note on single shoes. Comparatively speaking, the adidas shoes are easy. At least there's supposed to be a match! But in collecting millions of pairs of used shoes, we get lots of singles that will never pair up. Again, this looks like a problem, but even this is an opportunity if we dig deep enough—because there is a market for singles in places such as Pakistan, where we sell them for a few cents a pound. They are called "near mates." It might not be the exact same shoe, but they're the same size, and probably close in color and style. They pair shoes the best they can (it's a weird market—I warned you). We cover our expenses. We extend the life of the shoes. Somebody in Pakistan makes a little profit, and a Pakistani farmer gets to work in shoes that keep them safe. Not a shredder in sight!

We have another brand partner who offers customers a really generous thirty-day return policy, so when you are a company that sells millions of shoes each year, you end up with truckloads of returned shoes. Most are in new condition, but their policy is to give them to us rather than resell them at discount. This brand has grown in popularity, so they are in many more markets than they used to be, which makes placing the donated shoes harder; however, they don't have a presence in Moldova/Transnistra, so that's where we send a lot of them. Moldova is a poor country, Transnistria even more so, and it has been overwhelmed in recent years with refugees fleeing war, so people need affordable shoes and the orphanages are pressed to their limits. Because of the war in Ukraine, our direct partners have invested heavily in a warehouse and distribution center in Poland where they have purchased shoe cleaning machines, so everything they process exits their warehouse in nearly pristine condition.

As you can see, the methodologies we use to support the desired outcomes of these partnerships are quite different. This is true of all our corporate partner relationships. Each is unique. But all are united by a belief in the mission of putting shoes and apparel to work in order to improve lives and create opportunity.

There's one more thing that unites all the corporations with which we partner: *Literally*, we could not complete our mission without them. Without these partners, despite the unstinting generosity of individuals and community groups that send us donated goods, we would have so much less to put to productive use for people in need.

INDIRECT PARTNERS

Another group of partners we could not do without is our for-profit partners, or in our nomenclature, indirect partners and partners in practice and spirit. They represent a piece of a complex equation that isn't obvious at first to those outside S4S, and even to those on our team and board. Indirect partners have the scale and infrastructure to find viable markets for all manner of donated goods. For example, that ten-year-old, unbranded, corporate-logo polo you received at a fundraiser you attended but never wore may not have value to you, but it's a perfectly good garment for someone. When a company donates twenty-five thousand pairs of the same style and color of shoe, it would be almost impossible to move that volume to one of our direct partners. Their markets are usually too small, or the product doesn't fit (winter boots in Honduras?).

In the footwear and apparel industry, what we call indirect partners usually go by the unfortunate name "jobbers." Sometimes, they are unfairly painted with a broad brush because they move product that no one knows what to do with and pay pennies on the dollar. It's a very visible way of companies admitting that something didn't sell as expected, and no one likes to be reminded of that kind of misjudgment. Jobbers don't just work with small charitable organizations like S4S; the biggest retailers in the world have contracts with jobbers to handle the huge stockpiles of goods that didn't sell.

The word "jobbers" dates to the 1600s and refers to wholesale merchants who sell to retailers, and while this is an accurate description, it doesn't cover all that our indirect partners do for us. Because of their global presence, mature logistics, and vast industry knowledge, the best of our indirect partners help us keep our corporate donors happy by making sure product goes into markets where those corporations don't have a presence. The apparel industry is incredibly sophisticated at tracking product, and understandably, if a large corporation donates a shipping container of new, name-brand coats, it doesn't want the contents of that container to show up in a market where it sells those same coats. The indirect partners with whom we work today have the market knowledge and the integrity to have our backs in this regard.

It probably won't surprise you that such integrity wasn't universally true for all the jobbers S4S was using in 2012. Another reason that the jobber industry has an unsavory reputation is that some of them can be pretty shady, selling things in places they shouldn't in order to make the biggest profit, promises be damned. In 2012, we were desperately trying to rebuild our corporate relationships, and transparency was key. We had one jobber based in California, an established player who moved a lot of merchandise, who didn't honor our or our corporate partners' wishes. If a footwear company says, "We don't want any of our products distributed to Europe, Asia,

Australia, or North or South America," a good jobber will have connections that will allow them to send that brand's donations to Africa, the Middle East, or other markets the company has approved. In late 2012, when I was still trying to learn the names of everyone who worked at S4S, I received a phone call from an executive with one of our brand partners. With no small talk, he launched right into asking why jackets they had donated were showing up in Chile, a market they had specifically prohibited. We needed to be the kind of organization that could ensure that when we said we wouldn't place your product in Chile, then it damn sure wasn't going there. But this was one of the first wake-up calls I received on how we were failing on this front. Despite that jobber having a huge network, and despite being deep in the tailspin where every dollar mattered, we ended that relationship. Even though we took a short-term financial hit, we had to cut ties if we were serious about our values and being a trusted partner.

It was only a few weeks later that I got a call from a senior executive at a well-respected boot brand, a family business that had built a great international following. I needed an oven mitt for that first phone call because he was furious. We had screwed up in their biggest market outside the US. The problem predated me by months, but he (rightly) didn't care. His company had found product it had donated to us in an open-air market it had explicitly excluded. It sent its own employees in to buy up hundreds of thousands of dollars of its own product. And the company wanted repaid because S4S leadership had promised they would do so. But given S4S's financial situation, the company had ignored that commitment, and now it was time to pay the piper. We needed a few months to get the money we owed, but we did it. Understandably, the company never trusted us again. Overall, it took some time to sever relationships with a handful of jobbers and uncover the other problems, but doing so allowed us to concentrate on the partnerships we had with those who operated with transparency and integrity.

In the worst days of our tailspin, it was these principled indirect partners that kept us afloat. From 2012 to 2018, they were critical to our cash flow because, in those days, when we sold products to our direct 4Opportunity partners, it might take them three months to pay us (something that can still be true given the volatility in the places they work), but when we sell to an indirect partner, they pay us before the product ships. In the leanest of times, often they would advance us payment for product that we would not be able to ship for two or three months. None of these arrangements would have been possible were it not for carefully cultivated relationships with excellent indirect partners over a long period of time. In several cases, those indirect partner relationships go back to the very beginning of S4S, and I commend the original leadership team for initiating relationships with such good people. David did an amazing job of investing the time and transparency in developing those ties. Because they could begin to trust S4S, they were willing to give us the benefit of the doubt. While it's hard to put a dollar value on the "benefit of the doubt," it's an incredible act of generosity whenever someone does that for a person or an organization.

We're dependent on indirect partners because of the volume of donations we receive. And while we are small potatoes to them, the good ones don't treat us as such. It used to be that 70% of our donations were being sold to indirect partners and only 30% were going directly to our mission. With concerted effort, from 2019 to 2021, we succeeded in flipping that ratio, which of course meant shipping less product to our indirect partners. While this was spot on for our mission, it hit the indirect partners right in the pocketbook. In most cases, this would be a recipe for friction and tension. Instead, the opposite happened. They were invested in our success and understood why we were making such a change.

We learn from them all the time as well. Even though we were out of the woods on the day-to-day financial situation, we definitely had "scar tissue" that influenced how we worked. Our goal was to turn the inventory as fast as possible—there was no cash flow from product sitting in a warehouse. Yet, this blinded us to the fact that our indirect partners sat on inventory all the time! It was part of their tool kit. When Mike Shirey joined as our COO in August 2020, we were about to get a wake-up call on this front. On one of his first days, we received a giant shipment, and almost as soon as it came in, it went out. Mike asked, "What are you doing? What's in there?" We didn't know. We were proud of the volume we had moved. His response was, "Well, that's not how we're going to do it now." Because of his business background on creating value quickly, capturing market share, and streamlining operations, in his mind, we were essentially giving stuff away without knowing its quality. While we were busy patting ourselves on the back because we had cash coming in and could breathe from month to month, we weren't leveraging that new reality. Mike immediately saw that, by investing in more sorting so we could understand what we had and know its value, we would gain greater value per item. After implementing his suggestions, over the first two years, we doubled the price per piece. Now, we had more money for the mission! Essentially, Mike created an exponential revenue gain just by managing our product better.

Also, for the first time, over the last few years, we asked our indirect partners to make a financial donation to S4S, mostly for 4EveryKid, and they did! They make charitable donations not because they have to but because they are people with heart. They support our work in far less visible ways, too. For example, a few years ago, we had a group from adidas traveling with us, and their shoe donation was key to the trip. We screwed up, failing to give ourselves sufficient delivery time when the container was held up at Honduran customs. We called an indirect partner and asked if he had adidas product on hand or in the country. I don't know how he did it, but he bailed us out, saving the day with one of our most important partners. Transactional partners don't do that.

I'm sure there are other examples of this kind of candor and openness in what could be seen as purely a vendor/supplier relationship, but I'm proud of how we made sure to keep partnership at the core, regardless of what the value chain might have predicted. It's a bit of a cliché to say that people rise to your expectations, but our indirect partners have shown this to be true time after time. Some people in our ecosystem still aren't comfortable talking about this part of our business, but I will hold our "jobbers" up any day as people and companies we're proud to call partners. We've learned to share our history with indirect partners and be transparent both about why we need them and about the mission support they have extended to us. With a little education, people get it. I can look anybody in the eye now, including our most recognizable brand partners, and say, "This is why we have these guys in the system."

DISTRIBUTION PARTNERS

There's one other kind of partner we are very reliant on: those who have the logistical and infrastructural means for distribution in places we can't reach. They play an important role by distributing shoes and clothes across many of our programs, but they really shine in disaster areas through 4Relief. Whether it's in response to floods in Valencia, Spain, or hurricanes in the US, we rely on experts at disaster response and moving product at scale. One great example out of many is Convoy of Hope, based in Springfield, Missouri, but working around the globe. They have a wide range of programs serving women, children, and farmers, and have access to planes, trucks, and ships alongside logistics tracking software and vast experience. They work with nonprofits and fundraise to support their cause.

In some cases, even traditional charitable partners such as Convoy of Hope don't have an on-the-ground presence. In such circumstances, amazing team members such as Tiffany Turner step in and find a way. For example, in 2023, a devastating magnitude 7.8 earthquake struck southern and central Turkey and northern and western Syria. Getting aid to Turkey was manageable, but doing so in Syria, a country with a tense northern border and in the midst of a decade-plus long civil war, was challenging. After the enormous port explosion that happened in Beirut in 2020, Tiffany had made a connection there with the nonprofit group Ahla Fawda. One brand partner came forward with donated shoes and Ahla Fawda arranged for a local footwear company in Beirut to donate warehouse space. Since Lebanon and Syria have an open border, Ahla Fawda drove the shoes from the Port of Beirut to Aleppo, Syria. Here is the note Tiffany's Ahla Fawda contact sent to her:

> *First day of distribution, Hallab a city hit by war, followed by earthquake, is a city of rubble and broken souls.*
>
> *We distributed to families sheltered in a convent, (each room sheltering a minimum of 4 families) everything from food to scarves and shoes. It was rewarding and heartbreaking. The stories shared and the children's reaction from pretending bravery to the obvious fear and anxious faces … We obviously haven't seen, or experienced half of what people have felt and lived the last two weeks yet what little we experienced and saw*

brought us back to the Beirut 4th of August port explosion in 2020, and the dark days we are still living.

We are thankful to all our donors, our partners in this mission. Thank you for the trust. We care and will give care wherever we can.

This amazing example of the magic Tiffany managed and the brave generosity of Ahla Fawda illustrates how a lot of our partnerships evolve and adapt to fluid circumstances. These relationships bring life to what can be a banal term like partnership. It's helping each other, of course; but together, we do something that none of us could do on our own. Our brand partner couldn't get the shoes to Syria; Ahla Fawda didn't have the relationship with the brand; and we didn't know the organizations on the ground. And the people whose homes and lives were devastated would have been worse off if we hadn't found a way to weave all that together.

DIRECT PARTNERS

As you know by now, some of those people doing other amazing work on the ground are our direct partners. They form the backbone of 4Opportunity. They are the fuel that powers entrepreneurship in the places we have the highest impact. You have met Sam Darguin, seen the transformation he has accomplished through his organization HAC, and learned of the challenges he now faces trying to serve displaced Haitians in the Dominican Republic. You have met Raul Carrasco in Honduras, who, through his WCF, started small by providing opportunities for microentrepreneurs, and now has expanded to run brick-and-mortar retail stores and a warehouse that creates jobs and social opportunities. Both these extraordinary partners feature prominently in *Shoestrings*. While our direct partnership program has grown and evolved, not only in new places but within existing ones, our rebranding of it as 4Opportunity reflects what we have acted on from the start: a belief that opportunity creates more opportunity. There has never been a lack of will or an absence of hard work in places such as Haiti and Honduras. It takes incredible fortitude to just stay even most days. But through something as fundamental as selling shoes, we begin to change the generational cycle of poverty. As Raul says about the impact of providing small entrepreneurs with product to sell and advancing them the product as they start an enterprise, "The lives of these people, I think, will be different because they are *thinking* differently now." He paints a vision of the future in which the women who become entrepreneurs by selling shoes and apparel provide an example to their entire communities. "It is a future where their children are not just healthy, they may be able to go to college and lead different kinds of lives."

 ANOTHER VOICE | **Tiffany Turner**

Tiffany Turner is vice president, outreach for Soles4Souls.

Family

Over my time at Soles4Souls, I've watched partners like Sam in the Dominican Republic and Raul in Honduras transform from the experiment of "Let's try this potential business opportunity" to becoming thought leaders and respected authority figures in their communities. In Sam's case, having been forced by violence and crime to leave Haiti and instead help Haitian refugees in the Dominican Republic, every day he must face the reality that some of his entrepreneurs aren't able to open their shops on days when

> they are afraid to leave their homes because the police are in their neighborhoods, looking for those who are undocumented. Sam and Raul's side of partnership always includes such sacrifice, and even as they utilize their great business sense, they never lose sight of the impact of their work on the people they serve. They've not just grown their businesses; they've grown in character. They understand that, without the business opportunities they create, there would be hundreds of people affected who couldn't take care of their families.
>
> I have a hard time not crying when I think about them because I am so moved by their passion. I've traveled for S4S for the last eleven years, leading trips, and I have total trust in our partners. I would go anywhere in the world with them and never think twice. I know that we've not just formed an allegiance because they are partners in this work—they're family.

To illustrate the power of such impact, let's look at a very different kind of 4Opportunity partner, one that is so different that, as an organization, we sometimes struggle to include it with our direct partners. We had created a model with Sam and Raul that we'd become good at supporting and through which we had learned to measure the impact we had on communities, especially with their emphasis on entrepreneurship. Yet, what you will see through the following case study is that we're not creating a one-size-fits all approach to direct partnership. While Haiti and Honduras, Guatemala, and the Philippines are places where poverty and crime rates are high, each is complicated in its own way. Gangs, political instability, currency swings, and natural disasters are facts of life, but one size does not fit all—not even close.

5 POCKETS AND HEART4ORPHANS: A CASE STUDY

This is the story of our direct partner Mark Fashevsky, in Moldova—or more specifically, in Transnistria, a pro-Russia breakaway state from Moldova. And when I talk about every place having unique characteristics because of its culture, history, politics, economics, and religion, Transnistria is a category of one. It's especially tricky because Mark lives in a place where he is vulnerable to the whims of an oppressive kleptocracy, so there are aspects of his personal circumstances I won't reveal because I don't want to endanger him further. To understand the nature of Mark's partnership, you have to first understand some things about Transnistria.

Transnistria is internationally recognized as part of Moldova but has operated with de facto independence since a brief military conflict in 1992. It controls most of the narrow strip of land between the Dniester River and the Moldova/Ukraine border. Its capital and largest city is Tiraspol, where Mark lives. Its government and economy are heavily dependent on subsidies from Russia, which maintains a military presence and "peacekeeping" mission in the territory. Political competition is tightly restricted, and the ruling political group is aligned with powerful local business interests. Media freedom is restricted, authorities closely control civil society activity, and due process is a farce, driven by local authorities that carry out targeted, arbitrary arrests. It maintains its own currency, which is worthless outside its borders since no other government recognizes it. Some Transnistrians have Moldovan citizenship, but many also have Russian, Romanian, or Ukrainian citizenship. But if you only have a Transnistrian passport, it means you cannot legally leave. The majority speak Russian. It's a painfully poor region that is suffering under the collapse of Cold War–era industrialism. Employment opportunities are limited. The average monthly income is roughly $100 to $150.

Mark runs both a charity and a social enterprise. He is a businessperson, and you can probably begin to imagine how difficult that is in a place like Transnistria. It's almost impossible to get a mortgage or a commercial loan, unless you're in bed with the government. A difficult place has been made more difficult since the Russians invaded Ukraine, and Moldova, like much of Eastern Europe, has been swarmed with refugees fleeing the war.

Mark is originally from Odessa, so he's Ukrainian, but he grew up in Moldova. For a time, he lived in the UK, where he attended a Christian seminary. While in the UK, he saw the benefits of "Thrift Charity," thrift stores that fundraise for charities. Think of Goodwill or the Salvation Army. On his return to Transnistria, he saw pallets just sitting around that were filled with supplies that had come from charitable organizations, and that sparked an idea. Mark has always been devoted to changing the squalid conditions of the region's orphanages and improving adoption and foster care rates; so, in 2006, he founded the charity now known as Heart4Orphans. He saw the model of thrift charity as a way to support this venture. He's personally knowledgeable about the complexities of a region that produces a disproportionate number of orphans, mostly through migration, drugs, and alcohol, all fueled by low economic opportunity. He's focused on improving conditions for kids, single mothers, and families. In particular, he has tried to create a path out of the tragedy that awaits the numbers of girls who, at sixteen, are required to leave state orphanages and often fall prey to the lies of a better life sold by sex traffickers. Exactly the kind of long-term, big picture sort of social change and poverty reduction S4S loves to support.

Mark has been our partner since 2014, and is one of two partners spearheading an organization known as 5 Pockets. The first time I met Mark, he took me into his warehouse—a sprawling, ramshackle, unheated building that employed dozens. He had to buy it with cash because no bank would give him credit. He had other buildings where women were repairing clothes so they could be resold for higher prices. All of this was dramatically different from what he showed us later that day when he took us to his first store—a ten-foot-by-ten-foot basement space that looked like a dungeon. Today, Mark and his partner Sergei have fifty clean, modern, well-staffed thrift stores spread across Moldova, Transnistria, and Ukraine. We are his most important supplier of footwear and apparel. From our perspective, because he has such a large distribution network, and therefore the ability to take substantially large shipments, he is unique among our direct partners. Because of his scale, when Russia invaded Ukraine, he had the foresight to recognize how many refugees the war would create, and he leased, then purchased, a modern warehouse in Poland, which is where his partner Sergei is now based. Despite so many hurdles, at its peak, 5 Pockets created jobs for eight hundred people.

Ever the entrepreneur, when the refugees he predicted arrived in Western Ukraine and Moldova, he found a unique and humane solution to deal with the crush of people. Typically, in disaster relief situations, NGOs and nonprofits create a uniform system where people are provided a set assortment of clothing—a pair of shoes, socks, underwear, etc.—that meets their gender and size, and then it's "Next!" because the crowds are so large. Because Mark had a network of stores, he managed to create a system working with NGOs, the government, and others whereby, rather than waiting in long lines, refugees received vouchers that allowed them to enter 5 Pockets stores and choose clothing and footwear for themselves and their families.

Rather than adding to the trauma of being a refugee fleeing war, he created a system that offered them dignity, a way to get what each person needed, and a sense of normalcy. He didn't just show the nimble ability to help people when a crisis occurred; he did so with creativity and compassion.

Sadly, this is more than he has received in return. In July 2023, the Transnistrian government seized all 5 Pockets stores and shut them down, alleging that Mark and several of his team had committed financial crimes. Although they remain in a Transnistrian prison after almost eighteen months, none of them have been officially charged.

With Sergei managing the warehouse in Poland and the stores in Ukraine, they have been able to keep the business going, but at the time of writing, hundreds of 5 Pockets workers in Transnistria are still out of work. Meanwhile, what has been Mark and Sergei's response? You probably guessed it: They have increased contributions for relief in Ukraine to those who suffer through Russian bombing campaigns targeting cities such as Kyiv and Odessa. In 2024, Sergei, who had traveled to Kyiv to visit family, sent me a picture of the apartment block where he grew up. The building was little more than a pockmarked shell. A place that had housed civilians living their ordinary lives was now uninhabitable. And Sergei wants to open more stores!

The final piece of his and Mark's commitment is that they have continued to fund Heart4Orphans at a significant level, covered their legal bills, and paid 5 Pockets employees a reduced salary the entire time the stores have been padlocked shut by the government. Is it any wonder we celebrate this partnership?

ANOTHER VOICE | **Bernadette Lane**

Bernadette Lane is an emeritus board chair for Soles4Souls.

Reexamining Impact

From the moment I joined the Soles4Souls board, I heard of our long-standing partnership with Mark Fashevsky in Transnistria. Because Mark's model was so different from what we were doing with other direct partners, and because it was so large—with over forty-five stores and more than three hundred employees at the time—it took a lot of processing for me to find complete comfort with this partnership. I was eager to experience this model in person.

When the chance came to join Buddy and David on a site visit and better understand our impact in Eastern Europe, I jumped on it. Our trip included visiting a newly renovated two-story building that housed the offices, training areas, and short-term transitional housing for urgent/crisis situations for Heart4Orphans. We also toured a state-run orphanage. There, I saw how little hope existed for the children if they remained in such facilities; little hope, and no opportunity to break the cycle of poverty. Much of Mark's focus has been on expanding foster care in Transnistria, and in contrast to the state-run orphanage, we also visited the home of foster parents who, in addition to having two children of their own, had taken in five other children. The family environment was heartwarming. The children were safe and happy. I returned from that trip confident about the work of S4S in Moldova/Transnistria and the extent of our impact.

In a report I made to the board on my return, I highlighted three positive impacts:

- job creation as in a traditional employer/employee model;
- skills training as a path to employment; and
- breaking the cycle of poverty by providing opportunities for orphaned children.

Confident about the impact Heart4Orphans was having on children's lives and our mission to reduce poverty, I moved from skepticism about whether Mark's partnership offered a good fit for S4S to embracing board discussions regarding the possibility of replicating his business model and whether we needed to establish an additional means for measuring economic impact.

INTERDEPENDENCE

As you've seen, we have lots of partners acting in lots of different capacities. We are interdependent with them. Without partners and a partnership mindset, we would be stuck on the runway—with wings but no fuel for the engines. Your experience of partnership is probably different from ours; however, as an organization scales, it quickly learns that it needs others' expertise to assist it. I don't think any organization can be successful without trusted partners. Why not turn to those who excel at things that you don't? We're fooling ourselves if we think we can be the best at everything. And good partners often open doors we don't know exist. No matter your mission, when you take the time to develop long-term, reciprocal relationships—when you become a partner worth having—your speed toward moving your mission forward accelerates exponentially.

Without great partners, without the solutions they helped us discover, and without the lessons we have learned by working alongside them, S4S never could have considered tackling a new program that extends our mission in our own backyard. That's where we go next.

"STEPS" YOUR ORGANIZATION CAN TAKE

- Thinking about what it means to be a partner, internally and externally, can change every interaction. Looking for what is mutually beneficial usually leads to better outcomes.

- Not everyone wants to be a partner ... but you can still treat them like one. Some people and organizations are transactional. That's okay. Just because it's not mutual doesn't mean you become transactional too.

- Partnership is long term. If you're thinking in terms of months or quarters, you're probably not in partnership. We can now count our most successful relationships in decades. If your view of a partner is one-and-done, ask yourself what value it is actually bringing you.

- Sometimes, being a partner means you take one for the team. You might try things that don't work or don't work immediately. But if you have the right time horizon, it's not a loss as much as an investment in the long term.

- It's just better. I'd rather run the risk of being too trusting and open than playing defense all the time. It takes too much energy to always be worried about whether you're getting the short end of the stick. Most of the time, with most people, in most places, trust leads to more trust.

CHAPTER 10

Powering Change and Growth

Change is inevitable.
Growth is optional.
—JOHN MAXWELL

By 2019, we had spent more than a decade improving how we managed 4Relief and a half-dozen years learning how to generate growing, sustainable economic impact through 4Opportunity. We were financially stable. We had defined our BHAG and had embraced our north star. The flight path felt steady. But it was also a time marked by the change and uncertainty that came with losing our beloved colleague David Graben. And while we couldn't know it yet, a global pandemic was looming. Late 2019 also marks the moment when we began having discussions among the team and the board about expanding our programming. Those discussions eventually led to the formation of 4EveryKid.

4EveryKid is an audacious idea—a program that aspires to provide a pair of new athletic shoes to each kid experiencing homelessness in the US. "Audacious" is the only accurate word because the numbers are overwhelming. All told, somewhere between 1 and 1.5 million students (K–12) experience homelessness in the course of a school year, according to the National Center for Homeless Education.[2] This might mean tripling up in a house, couch surfing, or living in a motel, a shelter, a car, or on the streets. But any of these mean that a kid might not know where they're sleeping tonight. Students experiencing homelessness are more likely to drop out of high school. High school graduation rates for homeless kids are well below those for students who are poor but have stable housing. Not earning a high school degree leads back to a cycle of homelessness, representing the single greatest risk factor for experiencing homelessness as a young adult.[3] While many organizations are focused on the critical needs of food and shelter for homeless youths, school officials tell us that shoes are essential for students to succeed. Loads of research demonstrates that kids who receive new shoes have more confidence, attend school more regularly, and are more physically active.

ANOTHER VOICE | **Parker McCrary**

Parker McCrary is an emeritus board member of Soles4Souls.

Treating Kids with Dignity

From the time I joined the Soles4Souls board with the Dignity U Wear merger, I'd pushed for us to expand domestically. I was thrilled then when we began discussing what would eventually become 4EveryKid. The fact that in a country as great as ours we have kids who go to school and don't go to PE, don't engage, and can't focus in classrooms breaks my heart. Some don't participate in PE because they don't have underwear or they don't have sneakers or the shoes they do have are too small for them. When kids don't know where they'll sleep tonight or they're hungry,

---

2   The National Center for Homeless Education, https://nche.ed.gov/.

3   "The Issue," SchoolHouse Connection, https://schoolhouseconnection.org/about/the-issue.

shoes might not seem like a big deal. But they are. Everybody wants to fit in. Middle school can be relentless. These kinds of realities distract kids and remove them from the opportunity of an education. Having shoes might be the difference between whether a kid goes to school or not.

We've taken that message to heart. If we want to have kids be engaged in school, to learn and seize opportunity, if we want them to be productive members of society, we have to help them along the way. With 4EveryKid, we're truly providing a hand up and helping them to understand the value of education.

The idea that jump started what became 4EveryKid originated with Jaynee Day, who was the CEO of an amazing social enterprise, Second Harvest Food Bank of Middle Tennessee. Jaynee stepped down as CEO in mid-2019 after a thirty-year career guiding Second Harvest through incredible growth and impact. Beyond the work you might associate with typical food banks, Jaynee took the visionary step of creating a USDA-approved cook-chill facility, which let Second Harvest transform food donated in bulk, particularly from farmers, into shelf-stable products that soup kitchens and other agencies could use. It was a model we could relate to because not only did Second Harvest fill the needs of people facing food insecurity throughout Middle Tennessee but the ability to transform donated foodstuffs into prepared dishes with a two-year shelf life purchased by other agencies also expanded its impact into multiple states and provided the enterprise with sustainable, earned revenue.

After Jaynee announced her retirement, I was chatting with her as we left a Rotary meeting and asked her what she was going to do next. She told me that she was going to take a few months to clear her head and travel. Then she would figure out the "what's next." I had a simple request that would turn out to be transformational. I asked her, "When you're ready, could you help us figure out how to have more impact in the US?" So much of the long-term impact of S4S is in low-income countries. We often had questions from our team, individual donors, and corporate partners about how we could do more "in our backyard." Honestly, we didn't have a good answer.

Fortunately, a few months later, Jaynee said she was ready to dig in. After asking more about what we would be willing to do and how far away from our current model we would go, she went to work. After only a few weeks, she sat us down and said, "I know what you guys need to do." She told me how she had developed deep relationships through Second Harvest with schools in over ten counties. "I've been in these schools for a long time, feeding these kids," she said. "They have a donated backpack program, they serve breakfast, all this sort of stuff to take care of the kids related to school. I know that food and shelter are the most important needs, and we're working on that. But that's big and complicated. Clothes are important, but relatively speaking, easy to come by. The problem is shoes. They're expensive."

She's not wrong, of course. The cheapest athletic shoe you can find on Amazon runs about fifteen bucks. They are poorly made and don't hold up under the daily use of most kids. They are not a recognizable brand name, so they're "not cool," and as minor as that may sound, it's not. Our culture places a lot of value on athletic shoe brands, not just the price of a pair of those shoes, but in social status. We've probably all heard the sad stories of kids who have been killed over their sneakers. Indeed, a 2015 documentary titled *Sneakerheadz* concluded that 1,200 kids died every year in muggings associated with their shoes.[4] Let that sink in. Adolescents and children face tremen-

---

4   Marc Bain, "Fatal Muggings for Shoes Are Partially Due to Sneaker Hype, a Documentary Argues," *Quartz*, November 20, 1015, https://qz.com/554784/1200-people-are-killed-each-year-over-sneakers.

dous peer pressure and frequent bullying, and one important aspect behind such behaviors is outward appearance. It's always been easy to pick on the poor kid in the ratty shoes. Imagine the stigma attached to teenagers who are unhoused. They are often at the intersection of a lot of negative trends.

Adding to the price and status part of the equation is that, while there is federal assistance available to homeless families with schoolchildren through the 2009 McKinney-Vento Homeless Assistance Act, payments made to enrollees are capped at about $50 per child—that includes shoes. Good luck stretching fifty bucks to also cover clothes and school supplies.

Jaynee really captures the situation through a story first shared with her by Catherine Knowles, who runs the Homeless Education Resource Office in Nashville. Catherine told a story about meeting a little girl, Layla, who came to school wearing a pink cowboy boot on one foot and a pink flip flop on the other. From Layla's perspective—hey, problem solved; she found shoes that matched in color. The teachers and other kids didn't see her solution in quite the same way. How can that not break your heart?

Working with Catherine and her counterparts in other school districts, largely because of contacts Tiffany Turner had developed with 4Relief, we consistently encountered the message that the core of any approach should be providing shoes that made kids feel like they belonged, that gave them dignity and agency. We researched the problem and read the studies from experts connecting self-esteem and a sense of belonging to pride in personal appearance. We did our market research and discovered that no one else was working on this problem at scale. What we found paralleled our own years of experience with 4Opportunity all around the world—people care about their appearance. To see kids in poor countries demonstrate pride in wearing name brand athletic shoes is as common as witnessing their parents passing through muddy streets in high heels and dress shoes on their way to church. It's human nature. Self-respect can be buoyed by feeling good about how you look. Just as it does for you and me.

Jaynee was right in another aspect—theoretically at least: The problem was in our wheelhouse. Using shoes to reduce poverty is what we are all about. Yet, 4EveryKid offered new challenges. Scale was one. Distribution was another. But perhaps the largest was that the research clearly indicated that, to be successful, the program could only use new, branded athletic shoes. Even though we could get fine shoes manufactured for a low cost, this didn't meet the need these kids have to feel like they belong at the table. So, this meant that we would suddenly find ourselves in the shoe *buying* business, something with which we had no experience. And that, of course, meant that we had to be even more in the fundraising business, which was something that had always been a relatively minor part of our enterprise.

If those challenges were not enough, there was the logistical complexity of moving shoes in the least efficient way: a lot of recipients in batches of one hundred to five hundred pairs, which really drives up shipping costs. S4S was committed to covering those costs, not placing a burden on the schools. But that wasn't the end of the challenges. A huge part of sustaining dignity and agency is in providing a range of colors and sizes by gender. I can't describe to you how different this is from packing a sea container as full as possible with no regard for style or type. We were in a brand-new business!

ANOTHER VOICE | **Mike Shirey**

Mike Shirey is the chief operating officer for Soles4Souls.

A Chance to Learn

4EveryKid offered Soles4Souls a monumental entrance to the domestic market, even as it massively shifted the requirements for how we managed logistics and systems. Suddenly, we were shipping bundles of a hundred to two thousand pairs of shoes to individual school districts when we were far more accustomed to shipping by the ton. This created huge demands with a growth slope of outrageous scale—from 10,000 pairs of shoes in 2020 to a goal of 1,500,000 pairs by 2030—*and* tremendous opportunity for skillset growth. One of the amazing benefits has been for our Wadley, Alabama, warehouse team to learn a whole new skillset, and they have shined. As a result, in more than one way, 4EveryKid has helped us "grow the people." We've done so internally, and we've lifted kids' dignity as well. After all, we're not shipping "product" in the typical sense; we're shipping dignity and assistance.

COVID-19 had hit earlier in 2020, and our COO died in May. This was his area of expertise, and I felt lost. What I am proudest of, now that I have a few years' hindsight, and what I think may be most instructive about committing to growth, is that we made such a big decision at a time when it seemed like the worst possible moment to launch something new. During a pandemic and dealing with the death of a key executive was not the best time to add a new program that would totally change how we worked. So why did we? That's the interesting question. The obvious thing would have been to play it safe and focus on stability. The world was falling apart. But we made the opposite argument. I think it was entirely intuitive that, when presented with a problem that went to the heart of our existing mission, we saw that it mattered more than ever. The need was clear and growing. The entrepreneurial answer when discovering a problem is to find a way to solve it—to run toward it, not from it.

Doing the unconventional did not mean rushing in blindly. We had matured as an organization. We had learned from past mistakes, and we asked ourselves, "How do we responsibly put this into place?" We carefully considered approaches to mitigating the risk. As the idea took shape, we reached out through Bernadette Lane to her firm CCS Fundraising to complete a feasibility study. At this point, if I'm being kind, we had rudimentary fundraising capabilities. Our goal was audacious and aggressive out of the gate: We wanted to reach 1.5 million kids as quickly as possible. CCS led us through a process that tempered our reality about how fast we could get there. With their guiding hand, we addressed what such a program would require from our team: how we would source the product, how we would manage the logistics, and most importantly, how we would fund it. We hired a terrific VP of development, Theresa Miller, to lead our fundraising team. We were incredibly lucky to engage with Foot Locker, who was dealing with the retail meltdown in the US and around the world but still stepped up with a generous donation of $250,000 and 25,000 pairs of branded sneakers. No strings attached other than to go see if 4EveryKid would work. Have I mentioned what amazing things can come out of deep partnerships?

We had our first 4EveryKid distribution in October 2020. (I'd like to give full credit to our CMO, Rod Arnold, for naming the program. I had been using the objectively terrible moniker SFHK [Shoes for Homeless Kids], which I don't think I could have made worse if I tried.) Just as some schools were beginning to reopen, we showed up with these incredible shoes and a promise to keep showing up. We understood that to be successful would mean going from raising $1 million a year to raising $25 million annually to reach all the kids by 2030.

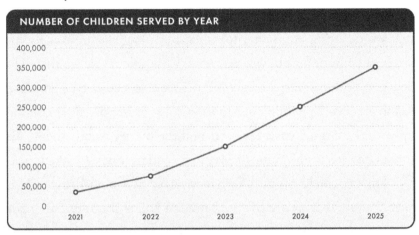

As intimidating as the logistics were, there was something bigger that we knew we had to achieve: creating mechanisms to accomplish our goal while demonstrating respect for the kids we served. It's not like you can drive a truck to a school and have them put an announcement over the PA system: "All homeless kids please come to the gym." Kids want to fit in, not stand out. The very intention is that, with a new sense of personal pride, they'll be able to stand out by the grades they make or through their participation on a school athletic team or in the school orchestra, not by being ridiculed for their family's financial circumstances.

By pursuing incremental growth in close coordination with school systems and liaison officers who specialize in assisting unhoused students, we were able to serve 35,000 kids in 2021. We have realized exponential growth every year of the program, and in 2024 we served 250,000 kids. The difference from 35,000 to 350,000, which is what we project for 2025, is monumental and has repercussions for the organization, particularly for our operations and business development teams. The prospect of figuring out how to reach 15,000 school districts is intimidating, but we remain committed. Our financial, inventory, and CRM systems didn't talk to each other and weren't scalable; so, in 2022, we began planning to implement an ERP system that would bring all of that together. Such systems are usually for larger organizations, but we knew that, without one, we would fail to deliver on promises to the kids and the schools, and maybe go broke in the process. Upgrading our tools was just as important as coming up with the annual goals for shoes and the money to buy them. We turned on Oracle's NetSuite in May 2023 and have never looked back.

I'm extremely proud of what we have accomplished but also keenly aware that we are still 1.25 million kids short of reaching our mission goal. If there's one thing that nags at me every day, it's that, for all the hard work so far, we still have so far to go. We entered with the assumption that we would get 30% of the shoes donated and buy 70%. We beat that projection in the first two years, and last year, in large part thanks to a substantial shoe donation from Fila, we flipped that equation and only had to purchase 30%. Meanwhile, a number of brand manufacturers have supported the program by giving us preferential pricing. With this kind of support, we have been able to keep our costs under $20/pair (which includes the shoe, shipping to our warehouse, packaging, and shipping to the school), in line with our original projections. We also saw that, to best serve the kids, every pair of shoes we give away is accompanied by a pair of socks—nearly all from Bombas, which is an amazing company that has had philanthropy baked into its business model from the start. It gives away a pair of high-quality socks for every pair it sells, and it has done this from the beginning. I can't say enough about the integrity, acumen, and commitment of the Bombas team.

When kids receive a package from 4EveryKid, they get shoes, socks ... and a survey—one more mechanism for tracking our mission, as do the McKinney-Vento liaisons. Alongside anecdotal evidence, which is so important because we hear from the kids and the teachers in such a direct way, the survey responses provide the quantitative evidence that the program improves self-esteem, school attendance, and engagement. Reading the survey responses and hearing about how kids perceive change in their lives moves us to do whatever it takes to continue to grow this program.

With each passing year, we forge stronger and stronger relationships. We are settling into a district-by-district approach. Each school district has a McKinney-Vento liaison, so there's at least one person focused on students experiencing homelessness. We've also seen extraordinarily generous, savvy donors support their home school districts. One extraordinary example is Rita Case from Fort Lauderdale, Florida. Because of the relationship Tiffany had built with Rita through her support of Boys and Girls Clubs, Tiffany had the opportunity to talk with Rita about 4EveryKid. She immediately got to the heart of the issue: How many kids in Broward County public schools experienced homelessness each year? How much would it cost? Could we make a commitment to a multi-year solution? Rita led with a personal gift from the Rick and Rita Case Foundation for $25,000 a year for five years. With her involvement, she rallied other community leaders and foundations in the space of a few months, who committed to $500,000 over five years. This meant that 5,000 kids in Broward County could count on new shoes until 2028! We have now implemented this model in Nashville, Dallas, and St. Louis.

We have a long way to go, and we are learning to apply lessons learned from this geographic model to other cities. Every community has unique hurdles to overcome. Reaching kids experiencing homelessness in an urban setting is not the same as reaching them in a suburban district, and it's entirely different in a rural one. Large schools are different from small schools. We have to factor in things like how different cultures feel about receiving shoes and how much storage space a school has. If we don't get the big and small things right, we create more work for the already burdened McKinney-Vento liaisons. The steady growth of 4EveryKid proves three things to me:

1. Doing hard things for the right reasons is worth it.
2. Preparation and mindset are as important as the business plan.
3. The right time is almost always now.

WHAT'S NEXT?

While we certainly identified risks in taking on 4EveryKid, primarily financial and operational, one of the biggest concerns was that we didn't take our eye off the ball with our other programs. Indeed, the continued growth of 4Opportunity has helped us recognize that generating a profit from this part of our work can actually drive us to reach the 1.5 million kids who need shoes even faster than if we only rely on fundraising. It becomes a kind of double flywheel: results for our entrepreneurs, direct partners, and the students we serve with new sneakers in the US. But one of our other existing programs is where we see huge potential: 4ThePlanet. This program is how we activate our commitment to sustainability for our partners and donors.

We've not always highlighted this aspect of our capabilities. Unlike Bombas, which built philanthropy into its business model from day one, care for the planet through sustainability was built into our mission, but it was not something we shouted from the rooftops. However, we learn from our partners, even indirectly. Seeing how effective Bombas has been in the last five years—at the time of writing, it has donated 150 million pieces!—we have leaned into 4ThePlanet, which we didn't even have a name for five years ago!

The environmental impact of producing, distributing, and disposing of footwear and garments is severe, and the industry focus on sustainability, while expanding, remains poor. It is an industry that is a notorious polluter, a significant contributor to CO_2, and a heavy consumer of water and other resources required to generate raw textiles; it can take 2,700 liters of water to produce the cotton for a single t-shirt, which is about what an average person drinks in two-and-a-half years.

The fashion industry's operating model is exacerbating the problem by stepping up the pace of design and production, particularly as more and more companies focus on "fast fashion," which is commonly defined as inexpensive clothing produced rapidly by mass-market retailers in response to the latest trends. The footwear and apparel industry thrive on introducing new products and new trends every season. Just think Paris or Milan or New York Fashion Week, trends created by influencers, or the onslaught of new, cheap goods from companies such as Shein and Amazon. Here are just a few highlights from a 2017 comprehensive whitepaper produced by the Ellen MacArthur Foundation, which features contributions from over one hundred experts:

- "In the last fifteen years, clothing production has approximately doubled, driven by a growing middle-class population across the globe and increased per capita sales in mature economies. The latter rise is mainly due to the 'fast fashion' phenomenon, with quicker turnaround of new styles, increased number of collections offered per year, and—often—lower prices."

- "Large amounts of nonrenewable resources are extracted to produce clothes that are often used for only a short period, after which the materials are largely lost to landfill or incineration. It is estimated that more than half of fast fashion produced is disposed of in under a year."

- "The textiles industry relies mostly on non-renewable resources—98 million tonnes in total per year—including oil to produce synthetic fibres, fertilisers to grow cotton, and chemicals to produce, dye, and finish fibres and textiles."

- "The industry's immense footprint extends beyond the use of raw materials. In 2015, greenhouse gas (GHG) emissions from textiles production totalled 1.2 billion tonnes of CO2 equivalent, more than those of all international flights and maritime shipping combined."

- "Less than 1% of material used to produce clothing is recycled into new clothing, representing a loss of more than USD 100 billion worth of materials each year."

This last bullet point from the foundation report highlights why an organization such as S4S matters so much, and is another reason why growing the footprint of our impact does more than help lift people out of poverty. It also emphasizes why our ability to influence change among our corporate partners is so critical. In developed countries, we live in a throwaway culture. S4S recognizes that your donated pair of shoes or piece of apparel typically still has a lot of utility. Simply put, just because I'm finished with a pair of shoes or a pair of jeans doesn't mean there's no value. That's a pretty privileged view, and I use that word very carefully. But after years of seeing how people with a different set of circumstances put those "finished" things to work, I don't have a better way to say it.

The fact is that when you donate your shoes or clothes, we extend their lives. Footwear and apparel that might otherwise have been prematurely discarded is put to productive use. Our research has shown that when it comes to shoes, we extend their lives by about fifteen months. This means reducing the CO2, chemical, and water impact per wear. In a world where there are no practical options to recycle 99% of shoes, getting them to people who can continue to use them is the highest use. While most of the time a word like "privilege" starts a fight, all I'm asking is that instead of throwing it away, donate it. I'd love for you to donate your used shoes and clothes to S4S. But if that's not for you, donate to Goodwill or the Salvation Army. If you want to make some money from them, sell them on ThredUP or Poshmark or eBay. Whatever you do, keep them in use as long as possible!

I hope you can see how S4S sits at the intersection of several contradictions. Our industry produces a great deal of excess, and S4S benefits from that, both from new inventory that goes unsold and is donated to us *and* when it gets donated as used. While there's tremendous progress on some fronts, recycling materials into new products remains technically challenging, expensive, niche, and (mostly) small scale. Still, while more and more footwear and apparel companies are paying attention to circularity, it's impossible to imagine a world in which there won't be a clear need for S4S or other nonprofits in the apparel reuse space.

So, there is commercial pressure to develop new products and sell more stuff. There is watchdog, legal, and consumer (the same ones who want the new stuff) pressure to be sustainable. It's hard to navigate the crosscurrents, but there are creative forces inside the industry that signal change, and we want to be at the heart of that. Relying on our value of being entrepreneurial and acting in the spirit of partnership, we have been able to be part of a sustainability option for one of our key corporate partners: Nike.

A senior executive on Nike's philanthropic leadership team asked Nancy Youssef if we might be able to help them. Nike had committed to taking back shoes through some of its US boutique retail partners but didn't have a great way to handle those returns. We leapt at the chance. It wasn't a lot of volume, but Nike was pleased with how smoothly it went, the shoes were amazing, and Nike made a generous donation to help with our work. High fives all around!

About a year later, as Nike was planning to roll out a take-back program in all its European stores, it asked if we could provide the same service. Starting with just a handful of locations, we're now supporting 250. Nike is focused on sustainability in their business. In Europe, its consumers are driving demand for greater sustainability, and EU regulations are drawing real red lines about waste reduction, including requirements for corporations to take responsibility for the end life of their products.

As we gained confidence, and the Nike leaders in Europe saw the results, they asked if we could deal with some of its e-commerce returns and unsellable items. We had already formed a partnership with Peter Erren, who owns Erren Recondition, a large-scale facility that cleans, repairs, and reconditions footwear, apparel, and accessories. Based in the Netherlands, his company specializes in working with companies around the world to return damaged, poorly packed, or mislabeled products to the marketplace as efficiently as possible, in the best condition possible. Most often, they are sold for full retail. Peter is the fourth generation of his family's footwear business, going back 130 years. Peter often says that the only things his company can't fix are the things it doesn't know about! I met Peter at an industry event in 2017, and he was curious to learn more about S4S. He spoke about the big picture behind his business of saving goods from destruction

POWERING CHANGE AND GROWTH

and protecting the environment. "I really like what you are doing at Soles4Souls. Can I help you bring that to Europe?"

Linking Erren Recondition to Nike has been a win for everyone. By providing the labor and expertise required for Nike's items that need minor tweaks, Peter and his crew get about 25% of what Nike sends them to commercially viable condition so Nike can put those items back into its commercial channels. Meanwhile, the Nike-branded product that doesn't meet the high standards for resale can be used in our 4Relief program, which is consistent with our program stipulation that it must be given away for free. Customer donations of used shoes and athletic apparel, which includes Nike and other brands, are available for our 4Opportunity program. What's totally unusable gets sorted for recycling. Nothing goes to waste.

Working together, we've been able to solve a business problem for Nike while helping them meet some of their sustainability goals. In addition to being a great partner, Peter has also been a European ambassador, making numerous introductions. He benefits because many of the companies he works with appreciate his affiliation with us and see his contribution to our mission as attractive, so they are happy to send business his way. Our ability to partner with a brand with Nike's status adds to our currency. Together, we have a straightforward, honest narrative about sustainability, *and* we really are increasing product life, all while generating an additional product stream that can contribute to our mission. Reduce, reuse, and recycle is more than a phrase to S4S; it's part of our DNA.

Innovation is at the core of what it takes to manage sustainable growth. In a social enterprise such as S4S, growth, ultimately, is measured in increased impact. Having a means to measure and guide such impact is where we go next as we close out our turnaround story.

"STEPS" YOUR ORGANIZATION CAN TAKE

- It's a cliché, but good ideas can come from anywhere. A former food bank CEO had a profound impact on S4S and hundreds of thousands of kids. Even big companies can need help solving problems—why not you? The main thing is to be open to hearing the ideas.

- "Clear on why, flexible on how" has served us well. I think being guided by big goals but not constrained by history or structure gives you the best of all possible options. Do all you can to have as many options as you can manage.

- I think people who use the phrase "We're building the plane as we're flying it" are nuts. That's no way to be a partner, a leader, or an employer. It's okay not to have all the details worked out, but people need to know they can count on you for the promises you make. It's good to take a leap of faith, but I'd be cautious about taking a leap into the unknown, at least if you want people to trust you the second time.

CHAPTER 11
Following a North Star

Fortune favors the audacious.

—DESIDERIUS ERASMUS

You might recall my telling the story of how, in 2017, David Graben and I sat down and, after many months and numerous approaches to gathering data, determined that by 2030 S4S could reach an economic impact of a billion dollars—our BHAG. As an organization, we had already settled on our mission of breaking the cycle of poverty, but that's very hard to measure. While we were well on our way to showing that the 4Opportunity program could legitimately claim to have aided in creating economic opportunities in the places we worked, we didn't have a way to include our 4Relief efforts, which are vitally important to our work. Our billion-dollar impact target was audacious and just this side of impossible. Perfect. But to tie it all together, we needed to connect that target with how we could use it in making strategic and operational decisions. We wanted a north star worthy of the name.

Historically, nonprofits have not been great with metrics. Most of them want to change the world, which lends itself to anecdotes but not so much to results. What usually ends up happening is that there is some big headline (End hunger! End poverty! End disease!), but what gets tracked is how many meals were served, how many people took the training, or how many shoes we gave away. Those aren't meaningless; they just don't tell you if it matters to those we're serving. For us, it was easy to measure the progress from collecting one million pairs of shoes to two million. That's the kind of metric that can make you feel pretty good about your work because it's freaking hard to collect 2 million pairs of shoes. That we had, by the end of 2024, received 107 million pairs of shoes and pieces of clothing is certainly worthy of celebration. It is not, however, a useful measure of impact. How many of these donations have made it to recipients in need? How many people have received more than one item? What is their dollar value? How many of those donations had passed beyond their life cycle? What did it cost to get them to the people who benefited? These are just some of the questions about using the number of donated items as a metric.

It's just as easy to get lost in the operational details and think those are the most important metrics. What percentage of donations went to our direct partners? What percentage to our indirect partners? What percentage went to 4Relief, where they were given away for free? What's the cost per container? What's the average price per item? Answering these questions is really important to running S4S, but you're not any closer to understanding impact.

David and I knew that supporting entrepreneurs through 4Opportunity would harbor more revealing information about impact if we could gain answers to the most relevant questions: How many jobs are created? How many people are dependent on each entrepreneur? What are their profit margins? Are they reinvesting profits? Does their presence attract other business? Are they displacing other businesses? Do they successfully recruit new entrepreneurs? What is the impact of work being done by our direct partners such as feeding kids, running schools, keeping young adults out of gangs, or creating a path out of the sex trade for orphaned young women?

So we looked around for the traditional tools that measure poverty and how certain interventions might change the rate and depth of those conditions. At first, we used a standard industry questionnaire tool that has been validated by many others. We employed it initially in Honduras, asking questions such as: Did your kids eat last night? Does your dwelling have a dirt floor? Do you cook on a wood fire? There we were, asking our questions in broken Spanish, all the while thinking, *How invasive and condescending to show up and ask people to tell us how terrible their lives are so we can validate our work?* We were a little disgusted with ourselves. There had to be a better way.

NEW METHODS

So we went down a more focused approach by working with Vanderbilt University's Master of Public Health program. We sent several graduate students to Haiti to live and work for a summer. They returned with a clear message that if we were to take this kind of approach, it would require people on the ground long term to establish trust. The entrepreneurs they talked to were suspicious that the data they shared could be used against them—if we knew how much money they were making, then obviously we'd raise the prices. It would be expensive, incomplete, and way outside our expertise. So back to the drawing board again.

David and I scratched our heads some more and kept returning to one fundamental question: What is a product worth to the people who benefit from it (regardless of whether it was provided for free or they purchased it)? We got entrepreneurial. We went to places where we had direct partners and asked local people to buy shoes. We asked them to buy as many shoes as they could, with quotas for different styles, with the caveat that they had to spend all the money we provided. They were incentivized to get the best deal they could because they got to keep a pair of shoes; and because we had others going out in the market and doing the same thing, there was an element of competition. Vitally, we got a sense of a fair market price—not the "American" price we would have gotten if we'd been doing the shopping! Starting in Honduras, we applied this approach in Haiti, Uganda, Malawi, Sierra Leone, and Nicaragua. We knew the prices we were getting from our partners, and they maintained data on what they charged entrepreneurs, and this tactic allowed us to know how much the entrepreneurs were able to put in their pockets (minus expenses for necessities like rent).

We understood that the highest economic impact came from working through our direct partners and the entrepreneurs they supplied. The second-highest value was in goods we gave away for free. Our lowest value came through the products we sold to our indirect partners because they were the ones making most of the money. We didn't count our piece in any of the valuations, only what stayed in the countries where the product ended up.

I want to be clear about the trade-offs we made in this approach, because it's not perfect. We sell shoes to our direct and indirect partners mostly by the pound. They sell them to their entrepreneurs by the box or bag. As they sort through the product, they maximize the price differences between branded athletic shoes (very high), women's heels (medium to low), and cowboy boots (pretty low). They are masters of dynamic pricing! Even though the US retail prices of those might all be the same, that's not how it works in their markets. While they might not give a damn about our metric for economic impact, we are aligned. We all want them to make as much money as possible so they can take care of themselves and their families.

As we dug into other data, crunched the numbers we had available, talked more, and thought earnestly about our growth trajectory and the future, it was with a mix of bravado and fear that we began to share discussions of the billion-dollar impact BHAG. Soon after, Robert Adams-Ghee joined as our CFO, and he was able to help us structure the goal and make it possible to report on it consistently. We were feeling good about the target and how it worked for us. Then, one of our board members asked a question that took us by surprise and changed how we really used our north star. Let me turn the narrative over to Bill Strathmann.

ANOTHER VOICE | Bill Strathmann

As a CEO, Bill Strathmann led, grew, and then sold Network for Good, a software company that provided fundraising and coaching for small and medium-sized nonprofits. Bill came to Network for Good from a background in management consulting with BearingPoint and Andersen Business Consulting. At the latter, he developed and led a consulting practice serving large nonprofits, including the Nature Conservancy, the National Geographic Society, the National Association of Home Builders, and the United Way. The former chair of the Social Enterprise Alliance, he is an emeritus board member of Soles4Souls.

A Compass Bearing

Buddy gives me too much credit for helping Soles4Souls clarify their north star. During a board discussion examining our strategic plan, I asked a straightforward question: "What percentage of the time do we go with an in-country partner who is actually helping lift people out of poverty versus just selling the shoes for revenue to a jobber?" At the time, the answer was 25-30%. I emphasized that this was a key metric we needed to measure. My experience at Network for Good working with nonprofits had solidified my belief that if they have an earned revenue strategy that could help them further their mission instead of simply being complementary to it, that's an extraordinary opportunity. Earned income can make every dollar raised go farther than an organization dependent only on charitable dollars. To put this in context, you can buy Ben & Jerry's ice cream because their values complement your own, but while their activism is philanthropic, it's not a fundamental furthering of a core mission. I believe that if you can solve a social problem with a business strategy, then there's kind of a moral imperative to do so. From the discussions prompted by my question, we next asked: "What's that impact now, and where do we want it to be in the future?" It was through these kinds of conversations among the board and the leadership team that we helped shape the billion-dollar impact goal—their north star to guide, and measure, future impact.

S4S represents a unique circumstance that provides even further leverage for each donated dollar because of the millions of dollars-worth of donated product it collects. It's not easy to build and maintain the level of supply chain logistics that Sole4Souls has done, but with it the organization has supplies that it can sell at a low price to mission-aligned partners in the 4Opportunity program. The combination of the donated product strategy with the mission-aligned earned revenue strategy creates a kind of super leverage because they have very low supply costs in addition to earned revenue covering part of their expenses.

The other half of my belief in social enterprise, like the unique model S4S had developed, is far more emotionally based and goes well beyond the financial impact of earned revenue. I was

> originally attracted to S4S's international scope and the mission, and once I got to witness the power of putting shoes on a kid's feet and saw their expressions of pride and confidence, I was hooked on wanting to be a part of this work. More than that, I saw how donated product had a ripple effect as it flowed into communities through the largely female entrepreneurs who sold it and created income they'd only been able to dream about. The impact of this social enterprise to reduce poverty was powerful—so much more powerful than simply selling product to jobbers. Our ability to measure impact allowed us to develop strategies that would elevate it each year.
>
> One of the biggest challenges among nonprofits is the difficulty of measuring outputs. In the for-profit world, doing so is easy. In an add-on piece to his book *Good to Great*, Jim Collins said that one of the dangers of nonprofit ventures is that if you don't have clear outputs to measure, then you consistently focus on inputs. You obsess over "How much am I spending on this stuff?" And that's why, in my opinion, so many nonprofit boards tend to be risk-averse. They are focused on the dollars going out because they don't have a good output measure of the impact they are having. Once S4S fully embraced the uniqueness of their social enterprise model and the full impact it could have on their mission, they found a clear north star, including developing the metrics to measure it, and following that course has led to steady growth.

I admit to being pissed off at first by Bill's questions. We were in good financial shape and were growing our impact. Why did he have to make it harder? But the conversations prompted by these questions made us examine how much we were really delivering on our mission … not just in stories but in quantitative results. We needed to make our direct and free channels the vast majority of our impact. We also had to examine the percentages between our use of direct and indirect partners. If we sell a pair of shoes to an indirect partner, who will keep most of the profit margin, we realize $5 of economic impact. But if we sell the same shoes to someone like Sam in the Dominican Republic, we create $15 of economic impact. The cash amount is the same, but the economic impact is tripled. There are many good reasons to work with our indirect partners, but they advance our mission the least. So, we created a system that essentially penalizes ourselves if we take the easy route and sell to an indirect partner because it forces us to move a lot more product to achieve the same impact.

This north star offered us the kind of guidance that we could use for strategic, long-term planning as well as in our day-to-day decision-making. This was the real beauty of our work on economic impact. It's a powerful accountability tool that can be used in a purposeful, transparent way. But we kept getting questions about how we created our model and the assumptions and math behind it. No matter how good we felt about it, foundations and more sophisticated donors didn't think the answer "mostly David and Buddy and buying shoes in the open market" had enough gravitas. By early 2021, in part because we were getting in front of larger donors to talk about 4EveryKid, we needed to take it up a notch.

Having continued to build the Advisory Council that came with the Dignity U Wear merger, we had many additional expert resources, including council member Deborah Weinswig, founder and CEO at Coresight Research. Knowing we needed third-party validation, we contracted Coresight to assess our economic impact model so we could make it stronger. We were fully transparent with them, sharing our data and our assumptions, and we essentially said, "Can you prove that this thing is valid?" After about three months of analytical and field work, they confirmed that our numbers were on target. "The good news is," they said, "you actually undershot the value." It was not until we heard their assessment that we realized how long we'd been holding our breath! We were thrilled that our instincts and practical approach had been on track, and relieved that we could move ahead confidently. We had the chance to go back and recalculate the economic impact for the entire time, but that felt like a shortcut. So, rather than recalibrate, we agreed to use the new validated numbers from July 2022 onward.

Coresight's analysis provided us with more insight as we embarked on 4EveryKid, which brought in new valuation/impact challenges. With the new, branded shoes we purchased for 4EveryKid, we knew exactly what we were paying for them. But the donated value was still squishy, and now we had to account for both in the same program. The big curve ball, however, was that even if we could point to a new pair of sneakers retailing for $100, that wasn't the impact. Nor was the cost of the shoes. And, we knew all too well that, for many of these kids, their options were hand-me-downs, a thrift store, or the cheapest shoes they could find online. We assumed that about 15% just wouldn't get new shoes; they'd keep wearing whatever they had. We are purposefully conservative in our impact measures. If the north star is to mean anything, we don't want to game it.

CHOOSING YOUR NORTH STAR

For some organizations, identifying a north star or a BHAG can be a "check the box" exercise. They set it in place and perhaps revisit it once a year during for their annual report. It's more a vanity metric than integrated into their work. That's not what we wanted. In part because we are trying to maintain our ratio of 70% of product going into our 4Opportunity, 4Relief, and 4EveryKid channels, our total impact metric is something we track all the time. Our operations team can tell you where we stand at any moment, and since it is part of our

FROM TAILSPIN TO TAILWIND

daily dashboard, it's on everyone's radar. Staying honest on the triangle of free, direct, and indirect means that we are constantly examining where the donations are going. For the executive team, which has the most influence on that triangle, part of our bonus is tied to it. We're not joking around.

Those outside S4S can find our north star confounding. I get it. Our economic impact metric is totally idiosyncratic. You couldn't take our model and transplant it to a different social enterprise such as a food bank. At the literal level, our north star might not apply to anybody else; but beyond the literal, having the means to track your progress toward an achievable, audacious goal should matter to every organization. Our north star isn't just a measurement—it drives our overall strategy. Our total economic impact has steadily risen every year and, correspondingly, so have metrics such as our revenue, net income, and economic impact per employee. These are not just indicators of being successful in advancing our mission; they demonstrate that we have done so while being good stewards, and being efficient with our product donations and with the dollars we earn and are entrusted with by our donors.

Will we achieve our BHAG and produce $1 billion in economic impact by 2030? You'll have to stick around and keep following S4S to find that out definitively. But what we can say is that we remain on track; as of the end of 2024, we have generated more than $698 million in economic impact since 2006. So, what happens in 2030? If the transformation from tailspin to tailwind has taught us anything, it's that the unexpected will arrive, new challenges will emerge, change will be necessary, and new faces will appear—and that certainly means we will need to formulate another BHAG. Having the right north star is powerful; almost magical.

As I write this, we're about five years away from that ambitious goal we set in 2017—a little more than halfway. But even now, we're thinking about what's beyond $1 billion in economic impact. The team and the board that has the helm then—it likely won't be me—will find a new BHAG. When we do, that will require new strategies and goals. But I don't know if it will require new tools. Ultimately, what has transformed S4S is everything this book is about: the quality of the team, the pursuit of core values, a business operating system, and the engagement of our board, among others. I believe those lessons will live on and will give S4S the best chance at being here for the long term. I hope you find some ways they can apply to you and your situation, and that you build on them to create your own flight plan to success.

"STEPS" YOUR ORGANIZATION CAN TAKE

- The north star or BHAG is a ten-/fifteen-year time horizon. This means you're going to live with it for a while. Take your time and make sure it's one you want in front of you for the long haul. You should have only one BHAG ... it takes that much focus.

- Your north star should fit your unique goals and strategies. It especially needs to speak to you and your leadership team. Your north star might use an industry standard, but don't limit yourself.

- For any strategy planning, usually in a three-to-five-year timeframe, it really helps to start with your north star. The more you ensure your actions are consistently oriented toward the BHAG, the more this sends the message to your team that this is nonnegotiable. If you can incorporate it into your compensation system, even better.

- The best BHAG keeps one eye on the distant future and the other on the day-to-day. The more you use it, the more tightly you weave it into the fabric of how you work. And that increases your odds of reaching your north star.

CONCLUSION

Finding the Updrafts

So, that's it. I've tried to condense the experience of the last twelve years into "lessons learned" that I hope you will find useful. Or at least interesting! It takes equal amounts of ego and vulnerability to make the case for "useful."

It's easier to recognize the tailspin than the tailwind. When the lights are flashing red on the financial situation or your team's turnover rate, you know. But as the indicators move from red to yellow to green, it doesn't always feel as though you're pulling out of it. Those later moments can be just as risky. The strategies and tactics that you need at the bottom aren't the same as those you need when you're stabilizing or once you are growing. To stick with the analogy of the title, it's appropriate for the pilots to freak out in the dive, but you don't want them only focused on avoiding a disaster. If they're not planning for what's happening five hundred miles ahead, that can be just as much of a problem.

Take the "W." One thing I know I would do differently is taking time to celebrate the wins more often. When you get the plane back to level, it's okay for a round of applause for the crew. My MO has been to focus on what's wrong, what we can improve, what's next. While that may work for me, it's not the right approach for the entire team. There's no question that I missed too many opportunities to recognize the amazing things we pulled off in all stages of pulling out of the tailspin and into the tailwind. There's a difference between thanking people, which I do, and pausing to call out the progress and success along the way, which I do less well. I think you need both. My one piece of advice is that, if you're wired like me, you should find the person on your team who has the celebratory gene and listen to them. Make the time. It's not a distraction to celebrate the wins—it's part of a leader's job, one that I wish I had been better at recognizing.

There is a time to let it go. We've heard from Milledge Hart a few times in this book. He's had a big impact on me, including when he holds up a mirror to things I don't want to see. One of the most important was telling me, without a lot of sugarcoating, that I had to let the turnaround story go. While I am incredibly proud of all that we have accomplished, at some point, almost nobody remembers or cares: employees who have no idea we used to sweat payroll; board members who don't know why we get giddy every time we talk about having a reserve; partners who just want to know what we can do now. The tailspin seems like it's in S4S's DNA, but it's not. There is certainly value in knowing where we came from, but, as the saying goes, you can't navigate the future looking in the rearview mirror. Hanging on to that story, those playbooks, can blind you to the opportunities ahead. I've had the good fortune to have a team and a board who make sure that doesn't happen. If you don't have such people in your ecosystem, you might be flying blind.

"Everyone has a plan till they get punched in the face." This is definitely not an airplane metaphor! Still, it's one of my favorite quotations, usually attributed to the boxer Mike Tyson. I try to put that into practice in two ways.

The first is that plans don't usually survive contact with reality. The market's changed; the team is different; you made some wrong assumptions; the spreadsheet turns out to be too optimistic. That doesn't mean you don't have a good plan, but that punch—and it will come—demands that you adapt. That's a key moment that every leader faces, usually more than once. How you respond sets the tone for your organization, so keep that in mind as you navigate the blows.

The second is that you think you know what's important, but until choosing the "right" thing costs you (money, time, reputation, relationships), you don't really know how you'll respond. Be ready for that. There were some relationships that we ended early on that made our financial position more precarious. We had long-term employees whom we asked to leave because they weren't aligned with where we were going even though they had worked with our corporate partners for years. Yet, not making that call would have inflicted far more lasting damage because people on our team would have, rightly, concluded that our values were situational: easy to talk about until the going got tough. PS: No partners left, because the connection goes beyond any one person to the mission.

And always remember that everyone is watching as you make those choices. Those are the stories that get told and retold; the stories that make up the most important, hardest-to-define work of a leader: culture. You are talked about with friends and spouses, over dinner and in bed before the light goes out. I have forgotten that at my peril in the past, and I work *very* hard to be consistent in what I say and do. S4S has taught me the value of that over and over.

Going it alone is a choice. Sometimes I get frustrated at the hero worship of the entrepreneur, or the person who says he doesn't owe anyone because he "pulled himself up by his bootstraps." There's a whole network of people and institutions around each of us that both holds us back and enables us to do great things. Putting so much focus on just one person leads to some dangerous side effects at best, and to some truly deranged beliefs at worst.

I don't say very much that's categorical in this book, but when it comes to recognizing how each of us is part of a community, I don't have much room for argument. You don't have to lead by polls to listen to other perspectives, to ask for help, to say "I don't know." While there have been times I have felt lonely at S4S, I have never felt alone. The people around me personally and professionally have been an unlimited source of inspiration and wisdom, at least when I've been open to it. Some of those relationships are the result of a lifetime of interaction; some come with the job. All of them take work, and I can only say that it would be hard to overinvest in those relationships. They will sustain you, make you better, and help you remember that you're important—just not the most important.

I cannot thank you enough for investing your time in our tailspin to tailwind story. But what matters most to me is that you found something worthwhile here, something that will help you when your own tailspin moment arrives, as it always does. And that a few of these ideas can be a part of you finding your tailwind. Onward and upward!

To learn more about Soles4Souls, go to soles4souls.org.

ACKNOWLEDGMENT

It's hard to know not only where to start the acknowledgements; it's hard to know when. Do I go back to my parents, who provided an amazing family and childhood for me and my siblings? Do I thank my high school AP English teacher whom I couldn't stand at first and by the end of my senior year I respected above any other? Or my college advisor who put me on the path to think about service? SMU for giving me a full scholarship, the only way I could have ever earned an MA in arts administration and an MBA? So "when" is super complicated, and I could have gone into a lot more detail!

Maybe the right decision is to stick to this book. My first shoutout goes to a former YPO colleague, Deb Zablodil. In 2022, in her role leading education for the American Society of Association Executive's five-thousand-person annual conference in Nashville, she reached out to see if I'd like to speak. I leapt at the chance, but I was going to have to work for it. She said that she didn't want me to just give the usual talk about Soles4Souls. Instead, could I go deeper and find something that was more universal than simply talking about S4S's work? The theme that year was "Disruption=Opportunity." I don't know if it was successful for ASAE, but it was a game changer for me. Because as I thought about Deb's charge to me, it seemed like exactly the invitation I need to think through the previous ten years. For as hard as we were all working, had we learned anything? That talk launched this book, and I will be forever grateful for Deb pushing me in a new direction.

There's also no book without the team I've been lucky enough to work with since 2012. Many are included in the book, but many more are not. Each person, partner, traveler, donor, employee, and board member helped shape the organization and me—both the positives and negatives—and we could only be here because of that complex web of relationships. It's been the experience of a lifetime. I have never been so engaged and fulfilled as I have since the day I walked in the door at 319 Martingale.

I'd like to especially thank Jamie Ellis, our VP of strategic communications. Her insight and experience have been integral to bringing T2T to life.

I'm also very grateful for the chance to work with Advantage Media | Forbes Books again. Adam and his team are pros. I especially appreciate the chance to work with Mark Leichliter ... Mark, the pleasure was all mine.

It feels weird to acknowledge two people who weren't able to add a word to *From Tailspin to Tailwind*, even though their spirit suffuses nearly every page. This book is dedicated to David Graben and Robert Adams-Ghee, but that does not come close to describing their impact on me and Soles4Souls. They are missed by many and will be for as long as I can imagine.

Lastly, any acknowledgement that doesn't include my wife and daughters is just insane. Their support is why I can do what I do. They are also very good at reminding me not to ever believe my own PR. We joke about it, but they have made me better in every way that matters.

ABOUT THE AUTHOR

BUDDY TEASTER is the president and CEO of Soles4Souls, a global nonprofit that turns shoes and clothing into opportunities for people in need. A passionate leader and advocate, Buddy has guided the organization to distribute more than 107 million pairs of shoes and garments across 140 countries, supporting communities through both immediate aid and sustainable microenterprise programs.

A dynamic thought leader, speaker, and author of *Shoestrings: How Your Donated Shoes and Clothes Help People Pull Themselves Out of Poverty*, Buddy has been recognized as a YPO Global Impact Award Finalist and was included in the *Footwear News* 2019 Power List. His innovative approach has transformed Soles4Souls into a movement that blends philanthropy with sustainable development, earning the organization recognition as one of *The Nonprofit Times*'s "Best Nonprofits to Work For" three years in a row.

In his free time, Buddy enjoys endurance sports, storytelling, and spending time with his family.

For more information, visit BuddyTeaster.com.

GLOSSARY

4Opportunity: In low-income countries, it's difficult to escape poverty because long-term work is scarce. Soles4Souls sells and distributes shoes and clothing through our international partners to help people build small businesses.

4Relief: When people experience economic hardship—either chronically or because of a crisis—meeting basic needs is a challenge. Together with 1,900+ partners around the world, S4S gets new shoes and clothing to people in crisis, freeing up financial resources they can use toward other needs.

4EveryKid: More than one million children in the US don't have stable housing, and their families lack sufficient resources to meet all their basic needs. S4S partners with schools across the country to get new athletic shoes to children experiencing homelessness. This gives kids the opportunity to participate more fully in school, and it frees up resources their parents can then use for other necessities.

4ThePlanet: S4S cares for our planet and for people by extending the lives of shoes and clothing that might otherwise have been prematurely discarded.

Economic impact: Economic impact is an internal business and impact metric, used every day as a decision tool to keep S4S mission-centric and honest against financial performance. Our goal is to create $1 billion of economic impact by 2030. What does economic impact capture? It is what beneficiaries receive in monetary value from the goods and services provided by our mission. All product that S4S distributes holds some value of economic impact.

Gifts in Kind (GIK): Gifts in kind, also referred to as in-kind donations, is a type of charitable giving whereby, instead of money, the goods and services themselves are given. This is reported, monitored, and entered on a monthly basis by the controller. However, GIK is generally not reported on S4S's financial statements, except on audited financial statements at the end of the fiscal year.

Squirrel account: This is a separate bank account into which S4S transfers a fixed amount of money each working day. This account takes care of projected annual needs, such as year-end transfers to the operating reserve, annual payment of bonuses (as earned), and other capital outlays.

TEAM: TEAM stands for S4S's four core values: Transparency, Entrepreneurial, Accountable, and Meaningful.

Wadley: Commonly referred to as the "Wadley" or "Alabama" team, S4S's largest warehouse is run by approximately twenty employees in Wadley, Alabama. This warehouse processes the bulk of new and used product donations and coordinates containers for all of S4S's programs: 4Relief, 4Opportunity, 4EveryKid, and 4ThePlanet.

www.ingramcontent.com/pod-product-compliance
Lightning Source LLC
Jackson TN
JSHW080801130525
84337JS00013B/108/J